What About Me?

A Novel Approach to Personal Growth

Jacqueline M. Dierks PhD

Copyright © 2009 Jacqueline M. Dierks, Ph.D
All rights reserved.

ISBN: 1-4392-3367-5
ISBN-13: 9781439233672

To order additional copies, please contact us.
BookSurge
www.booksurge.com
1-866-308-6235
orders@booksurge.com

For my mom, the best teacher I ever had

author's note: This book is both a novel and a self-help book. It can be read easily for entertainment, or it can be read more seriously for personal growth. Unlike other self-help books, the advice provided in this book takes place within a fictional context. Although the characters are not real people, they have the same problems that many people face in today's world. This approach is meant to allow you, the reader, to see how to apply the advice given to the protagonist to your real-life experiences. You can experience the difficulties and successes that the main character, Samantha, encounters in implementing the new skills she learns in therapy.

As Samantha takes the journey of her life trying to 'find herself,' perhaps you can hitchhike along with her. The handouts that therapist Maggie DeWitt gives to Samantha in the chapters of this book are in the appendices. It is my hope that you will use them to create a more conscious, aware life for yourself. This method does work. You will also find, as Samantha does, that it means a lot of work on your part. Do as much or as little as you want. If at any time your feelings seem like they are overwhelming to you, I would advise you to contact a therapist.

This book is in no way a substitute for therapy. It is a book to encourage personal growth. If you are trying to improve your life, this book may be a vehicle that can help you. Many of my clients have said that they felt their lives were improved after only a few sessions because of the model that Maggie uses with Samantha. Some of the people who have read this book have reported that they see themselves and their lives differently after reading it.

This book is the first in a series addressing various problems facing women. An excerpt from the next book is at the end of this volume. The approach to personal growth in this book is one that I developed while working on my doctoral dissertation. I use this model extensively in my clinical practice, spanning 25 years working primarily with women. The client depicted here represents no one client and is purely a product of my imagination. If you are interested in the type of therapy that Dr. Maggie DeWitt practices, you would be well-advised to try to find a therapist who has training in both Gestalt Therapy and Cognitive Behavioral Therapy.

I want to thank my husband for his continued support and encouragement, and also my son and daughter for their unequivocal belief in me. Thanks also to Melissa Charman for her editing skills and Casei Malone for her graphics expertise.

    Jacqueline M. Dierks, Ph.D., LCSW
    Flagstaff, AZ
    jdwphd@npgcable.com
    March, 2009

chapter 1

"WHAT IS IT now?" I yelled as I walked through the front door—slamming it really hard so everyone knew I was pissed. *Absolutely everything is a crisis with my mother! Jesus, can't anyone just call me and say, 'How are you? How's your day going?' No, it's always a goddam crisis!*

My mother was in the kitchen, sitting in "her" chair at the kitchen table crying. This was her signal to the world that she was in 'crisis mode.' She looked pathetic, her head in her hands.

"What happened?" I asked, bringing my volume down an octave. My mother does that to me—the minute I see the sad face and especially the tears—I am 4 years old again trying to take care of her. *God, why did I have to be born into this family? What had I done wrong in some other life? Maybe I was the one who assassinated Lincoln or something, and I was supposed to suffer, big time, forever.*

"It's Brian," she said, her voice quavering.

Gritting my teeth, I said, "Oh God! What now?" *Saint Brian can't have done something wrong*, I thought to myself. Brian was my brother, two years younger, the last child and the only boy. He is tall, good looking, and easy going—another way of saying 'lazy slob.' All those things gave him the status of a saint in this house.

"He's met someone," she said, finally able to control herself enough to talk. She wiped her eyes and nose with her apron.

My mother is probably the only woman in the 21st century who still wears an apron. I'm pretty sure she made it herself, too. The funny thing is that the apron is perfect on her. It 'fits.' She still gets her hair done every week at the same salon, by the same woman, using the same pink plastic rollers, as she did when I was a kid. The outcome is a brown, curly 'helmet' that sits on her head like plastic from one week to the next.

She says that when she needs new clothes, she just goes to the back of her closet. She has stuff in there from the beginning of time—never throws a thing away. Her belief is that everything comes back in style. *Please God, don't let me turn into her.*

As I stood there looking at her with my hands on my hips, all I could muster was, "You called me, hysterical, for this? I left my pizza alone with Sarah because Brian met someone." I was truly amazed at my mother's ability to create a crisis out of nothing. "Mom, what is your problem? Why do you do this to me?" She continued to sob but seemed to be trying to get control.

She looked at me for the first time since I'd come in. Her face took on a look of pure disdain. "My God, Samantha, you look awful! Don't you care about how you look? How could you leave the house like that? I just don't know where I went wrong with you?" She just sat there, shaking her head.

I felt like I'd been punched in the gut. I looked down at my 'uniform,' sweatshirt, jeans, and flip-flops. I guess it was the catsup and relish I had spilled down the front of me at lunch that was getting to her. "Mom!" I shrieked. "You are the one who called crying, just sobbing on the phone. I thought something terrible had happened! Give me a flipping break!" I stuffed my hands into my jeans pockets so I wouldn't wring her neck.

"Watch your mouth, young lady! You know I hate swearing. I only called you because your sister wasn't home," she sniffed.

I should have guessed. I am always second best after my sister Kay. Kay is the oldest by a year, married to a perfect guy with two perfect children, living in a perfect house—the only woman I know, with kids, who can effectively carry off being both virgin and martyr without looking like an idiot. But that's Kay. She can do anything. "Where's Kay?" I asked, trying to act like I cared.

"She and Mike took the kids out on the boat," she responded with an accusing look that said, 'If you would talk to your sister, like you're supposed to, you would have known.'

"And you forgot there's such a thing as a cell phone?" I asked, using the special sarcastic tone that I save especially for my mother when she is clearly telling me something is terribly wrong with me.

"She said they needed 'family time' so I didn't want to bother her, and you don't need to be sarcastic. I'm your mother."

Like I could forget that fact even for a moment. The problem is that it never *feels* like she's the mother. I always seem to be mothering her. If she has a problem with Kay, Brian, Dad, Grandma, or the neighbor's cat for that matter, she calls me to complain. I know it works both ways. She calls all of them to complain about me so, basically, I just never tell her anything about my life. Unfortunately, she doesn't seem to notice or care that she's the only one who gets to complain. I just listen, doing my 'dutiful daughter' thing. Of course, inside I feel like I'm going to explode. Every time I interact with my mother, my shoulders feel like slabs of brick, my stomach feels like I've swallowed a rock, and just generally I feel like I want to throw up. *God, it's great to be home!*

"Okay, so what's going on with Brian?" I plopped into a chair after grabbing a couple of cookies to tide me over while I listened to her vent. *Oh my God! I'm inviting the tirade. What an idiot I am! Maybe there is something wrong with me—maybe she's right!*

"I told you, he's met someone," and the floodgates opened again. It seemed to me like she was making way too much of this. But hey, I'm not a mom so what do I know? "You aren't a mother, so you would never understand," she snapped. "I should have known better than to call you." She continued to weep into her wad of Kleenex. We should have stock in that company the way she goes through them when she creates a crisis.

"Mom, he's 28 years old!" I practically screamed at her. "You and Dad had three kids by now. What do you expect? He's got to get a life one of these days." *God knows, he's been postponing it for as long as he can*, I thought to myself.

Mom and Dad believe that until he gets married, he should live at home, paying nothing, so that he can save his money. So far, I hadn't heard anything about any money being saved. All I see is Brian going out drinking every night with his buddies, doing pretty much anything he wants to do, and Mom and Dad supporting him. Nice deal if you can make it work. You have to ask yourself, though, how many women are going to be interested in a guy who still lives with his parents?

"He's just so young," she replied. She seemed to deflate as she said the words. "You know what they say, 'A son is a son until he takes a wife…,' I just hate to think of him leaving. He's my baby," she concluded with a deep sigh.

"Mom, how many dates has he had with this woman?" The exasperation in my voice was evident. I felt like I was spitting the words instead of speaking them.

"I don't know—a few I guess, but you just never know. This could be the one, and I'll lose my baby."

She was heading off into catastrophe-land again, and I didn't want to be part of it. I was also pretty sick of hearing about her 'baby.' "I've got to run—remember I've got that pizza waiting for me. Next time you call, please don't just cry on the phone. Say something, so I know no one is dead." I was out of there!

Every time I walk in the door of my childhood home, it is like moving through a time warp and a jolt to my system. It's the eighties all over again. A pile of memories come tumbling back—most of them bad. The kitchen table is the same one that my brother, sister and I spread a two-pound jar of grape jelly on when we were little—of course I got blamed for it.

6

The living room remains a shrine—no one was *ever* allowed in there. My mother kept telling us that the living room was for company. In my lifetime, no one had ever been allowed in there. When I was little and learned that the British had a royal family, I figured that maybe if *they* came to visit, she would let them go in there. Well, they never came to visit and no one has set foot in there. Everything is museum 'perfect.' My dad and mom had a motto: "Buy good and buy once." These people really walked their talk. Just walking in the house makes me feel crazy because nothing changes—ever—not the people, not the things. It is no wonder that every time I leave, I feel like I'm escaping from something.

When I got to the car, I started to cry. I felt exhausted and half sick. I didn't care what the people who saw me thought. I was screaming at my reflection in the rearview mirror. "Why do you let these people, especially your mother, get away with this shit? I am a competent woman when I'm at work. I'm a supervisor. People actually ask my opinion. They listen to me and do what I suggest. They think I have a brain and treat me with respect. Why do I turn into a bumbling 4-year-old with her? Why does everything have to be about her? Shit, what about me? Don't I matter at all?"

I pulled myself together and actually drove the rest of the way home. It felt better than just aiming the car and hoping. All those tears made it really hard to see. I trust Lizzie, but she can only do so much. Lizzie is my car. I bought her when I was twenty-two, fresh out of college. She is a Honda Civic and was considered 'slightly used' when I bought her. She was all I could afford, and we bonded immediately. She is like a friend and seems to know her way home without me. By now she is well beyond 'slightly used,' but she's mine. She was my first real purchase on my own. I've never missed a payment or an oil change. I can do some things right, contrary to what my mother thinks.

I feel like such a mess in so many areas of my life. I'm closing in on thirty with no man in sight, living with my best friend from high school, and feeling like a total loser. *How did I get here? It all happened so fast. Geez, it was just yesterday that Sarah and I were graduating from high school and then college.* She and I have done everything together. She's the one who held my head when I puked my way through my freshman year of college because I couldn't drink but didn't want to be perceived as 'different' so I drank anyway. She's been the only stable influence in my life. She knows my family and how crazy they are, and she knows me and how crazy I am—and she loves me anyway.

I'm the one who has the "perfect family," just looking at our circumstances. At least, I still have my mom and dad. Sarah's mom and dad had been killed in a car accident when she moved here to live with her grandmother. That's when we met. She started high school with me our freshman year, and we have been inseparable ever since.

Everyone used to kid us when we hung out together. Sarah is tall, thin, and blonde. I'm short, 'big boned,' and brunette—good body, but nobody would ever accuse me of being petite. Sarah was athletic and really good at everything she did. She also happened to have the most beautiful, soft, blue eyes you have ever seen. She was just sweet to the core. Even though we were the same age, she always treated me more like her little sister. She was very protective of me, in a good way. I think my big, brown eyes make me look like a lost puppy to people. Sarah just sort of adopted me.

We both went out for sports. I only did it because Sarah made me. She always made the first team; I sat on the bench. I didn't really care because I really wasn't nuts about sports anyway. I just really liked being with Sarah. She made me feel good about myself—like I was normal.

Sarah always encouraged me to try harder. She believed in me. I didn't want to try harder because even though I had the body for it, I didn't have the brain for it. I liked to read and think and over-analyze everything. Sarah would just laugh at me and tell me I was too serious. Athletics were easy for her, because she really loved to play. Play was a foreign concept to me.

I pulled up to our apartment, knowing the pizza would be gone. My stomach was in such a knot that I probably couldn't have eaten anything anyway. Sure enough when I walked in, Sarah and our golden retriever Shiloh looked at me like I was from another planet.

"I thought sure you would stay for dinner," Sarah said contritely.

I had such a huge lump in my throat that I couldn't manage a response. There was no way I could be mad at her anyway. She looked so cute in her pj bottoms and t-shirt. Everything she owned had blue somewhere to match her eyes. What a cutie-pie. Oval face, blonde hair, great personality, all the things most women wish they had. It felt good to be home.

Shiloh, of course, didn't even have the decency to look sad or contrite. She was curled up at Sarah's feet looking extremely satisfied, licking the remnants of the pizza off her mouth.

"How'd it go?" Sarah asked. She knew by my tear-streaked face and red eyes the answer to the question, but she also knew me well enough to know that I would talk about it when I could.

After a few minutes of false starts, the words came tumbling out. "It's always the same old crap. Why does she do this to me?" My lip started to quiver as I looked to Sarah for some wisdom. She was the grounded one. She seemed to be so happy even though she, too, was turning thirty and single. "I just don't want to do this anymore. I am fed up with all the craziness. It's like living on a roller coaster—I want to get off. What am I going to do?" I felt like I was going to come unglued.

Sarah studied me for a while. She seemed to be turning something over in her mind that she wanted to say, but she just wasn't sure how to go about saying it. She looked weird, sort of scared. I waited. "Hellooo," I said, in my wiseass voice. "Anybody home in there?"

Sarah looked at me for a second or so and then started, speaking cautiously. "Sammy, I've seen you upset by your family for years. I know your family, and I love them. In some ways they have been my family too. I also really care about you and want you to be happy. One of the reasons that I'm fairly normal is because I've done a lot of therapy. I can't answer your questions. Just talking to me about your family isn't doing it for you, girlfriend. You need to talk to someone who can actually help you."

"I've been listening to you for years. Don't get me wrong," she grabbed my hand as she continued. "I don't mind listening, but I just can't do anything, and it is very frustrating for me. You need to find someone who can help you figure out what you want and need. You are so involved with them that you can't even see yourself anymore—if you ever could. There is no Sammy. There is only the person you try to be for them."

"Ouch," I said. "That hurt." What happened to my friend who's always on my side? If Sarah turned against me, I didn't think I could stand it. I sunk lower into the couch. I was hoping I could just disappear, which isn't a stretch with our old couch.

"Okay, okay, what's going on in there?" Sarah was clearly concerned. "I know you too well, girlie—when you get quiet, you're not okay. What's going on?"

Thankfully, one of Sarah's best qualities is that she is persistent. She won't let me just clam up and go away—she comes in after me. Tears welled up, even though I was fighting really hard to keep them down. "You are never mean to me," was all I could think to say and started to cry in earnest.

Sarah was by my side in an instant. "Oh, Sammy, I wasn't trying to be mean," she murmured. "I just really love you and absolutely hate to see what they do to you. You end up feeling like a pile of crap when, in fact, you have done nothing wrong. You turn yourself inside out for these people, and they don't see it or appreciate it. You deserve better from them and, frankly, from most of the people you are involved with."

That was a subtle reference to all the lousy men I've dated. I'm not a stupid person. I could feel Sarah's support but continued to cry. I just couldn't seem to stop the tears.

What the hell is going on with me? Why now? This can't all be because my mother is acting like her normal self. I tried really hard to drag myself back under control. It seemed like every time I tried to get control, I cried harder. *What the hell, let it go!* The only thing that made any sense to say was, "I think I just need a good cry."

After a while, I did get control. After a few good nose blows and some water splashed on my face, I felt human again. *Therapy! Holy shit! Nobody who's sane goes to therapy!* "Okay, my friend, are you saying you think I'm going crazy?" I asked the question tentatively, because I was honestly afraid of the answer. Sarah was looking at me with so much love that I wanted to just tell her to hug me and forget the whole thing. At the same time, I needed to hear what she was really thinking.

Sarah looked at me with a big grin on her face, "Oh, for Pete's sake, you goofball, I don't think you're crazy. I think you need an unbiased, third party who can help you figure out how to deal differently with your family." Sarah lowered her voice, "My therapist helped me to deal with my parents' death, but she also helped me to learn to deal with Granny. It was no joy ride moving in with her. You should remember that. We had our problems, but I learned and she learned—because we went to therapy together—how to deal with each other in good ways. You saw some of the rough times, but after a while things got much better. Even now, Granny is my rock, and she's in her eighties. We learned together. Therapy isn't just for crazy people. It's for people who feel like they are crazy *because* of the other people in their lives. You are one of those kinds of people."

"I'll think about it," was my hasty and only response. The thought of therapy was terrifying. I'd heard horror stories about how therapists make you talk about your life and how you *feel* about it—Yuck! The knot in my stomach had returned.

"Yeah, right!" Sarah said. She was clearly exasperated in her with me. "Never to be brought up again, I'll bet." She picked up the pizza box and smashed it into the trash can to emphasize her point.

"I know that walk. You're pissed," I muttered defiantly.

"I'm not pissed," Sarah sighed as she gave a sad look. "I'm just exhausted. Your family wears *me* out. I think I want you to go to therapy so that something changes. I can't help you. I've suggested everything I can think of, and it hasn't gotten any better." Sarah threw her hands in the air. "I don't know what to do or say any more, Sam. I want somebody to help you so that you stop suffering. Every time you have to deal with them, you either end up crying like you are now or so angry that you want to kill them—taking it out on us, I might add." Shiloh hid behind Sarah as if to reaffirm her statement.

Sarah seemed to take a cue from Shiloh and lowered her voice. "I'm begging you—call somebody," her voice trailed off. With a shrug Sarah added gently, "Let's just drop it for now. I'm really tired and need to get up early for work. I'm going to go read so that I can unwind before bed. I really do care about you, Sam." She gave me one of her big hugs. Then, she turned and went into her room, and quietly closed the door.

"Well, this is a fine howdy-do. It's 9:00 p.m. and there's nothing to do but think," I said to no one in particular since even Shiloh had decided I was not fit company and followed Sarah into her bedroom. I felt really confused and sad. *How had I gotten here? Maybe if I was asking that question, that was part of the problem—I didn't know how I got here. I'd just gone with the flow, done what I thought I was supposed to do to please everybody else.* "That's just great. I don't know who I am or how I got here—great!" *Now I am going nuts, and I'm talking to myself.*

I turned off the lights and headed for my bedroom. The idea of therapy was scary but also somewhat exciting. I needed to think about all this.

chapter 2

I FOUND THAT thinking about therapy for one night did not really do it for me. I'd been thinking about it for six months since then, and I still had come up with nothing. I had talked to several people and was really surprised by their reaction. Several of my friends had actually been in therapy—unbeknownst to me. Many of my friends were supportive, and those who knew my family seemed especially supportive (if not down-right euphoric) about the idea of me going into therapy.

I got several names and once in a while I heard a name that I had heard before, so I was actually getting closer to making the call. I'm a scaredy-cat though. What was I going to say to this person? How do you begin something like this?

It was a slow day at work so when my mother called, I actually had the time to listen to her complain about my dad and grandma for at least half an hour. When I hung up the phone, I grabbed the phone book and looked up the phone number of the therapist whom several of my friends had suggested. I'd had enough. These people really were going to send me over the edge.

I dialed the number, praying that no one would answer. Of course I heard the crisp, "Doctor DeWitt's office, how can I help you?" after only one ring. *Shit!*

"Hi! My name is Samantha Daley. I was hoping to make an appointment with Dr. DeWitt."

"Do you need evening appointments, or can you do one during the day?" the very pleasant-sounding young woman asked.

"Actually, I have a pretty flexible schedule during the day as long as I can plan in advance." *What am I going to tell Joann about my disappearances?* Joann is my boss and tolerates me because I do a good job. She has never been pushy about my schedule, so maybe I was trying to manufacture an excuse. *I could always take an early or a late lunch. That would work.* "Could I have something either before or after lunch? I think that might be easier for me."

"Sure," she responded brightly. "How does a week from Friday at 11:30 a.m. work for you?"

"Oh, that's just great. I'll take that." I wasn't sure if she caught the sarcasm, but I know I didn't sound very enthusiastic. I'm sure I sounded more like a woman on her way to a witch trial or something. After giving her all the pertinent data regarding insurance, I hung up and went to the bathroom to puke.

"What am I doing?" I was pacing the women's john, wringing my hands, and talking to myself (unless someone else was in there with me—God, I hadn't thought to check under the doors). If I didn't know myself better, I would think that I was having a panic attack. *This makes no sense—I haven't even seen the woman, and I'm having a panic attack! The idea of seeing her is making me sicker than anything I could possibly talk about.* "Why am I doing this?" I said out loud.

"Because if you don't do it, you'll drive us all crazy," came my co-worker's voice from behind one of the doors.

"Oh, my God!" I yelped. "You all know I'm going nuts!"

Janet, the woman who worked in the cubicle directly beside me and one of my best friends at work, came out of the stall and looked at me. "Sam, it's okay. I heard you on the phone, both with your mom and then on the call to the therapist's office. It's hard not to overhear. I wasn't eavesdropping, I promise. I could just tell by what you were saying that you were making an appointment. By the way, from what I've heard in the past and from what I heard of the conversation you were having today with your mother—it's high time."

I've been there, by the way," she continued. "When I went through my divorce, I saw a therapist. She saved my life. I swear I'd be in jail if it weren't for her. I wanted to kill the SOB, but she kept me sane through the worst time in my life. Go see the therapist, Sammy. It's the best thing you'll ever do for yourself. Besides, you'll be easier to work with." She washed her hands and gave me a big hug before she walked out the door.

Okay, so maybe I could do this 'therapy thing' a week from Friday.

When I walked into the therapist's office, my hands were sweating and I thought I was going to be sick. I had made it here! Everyone who knew I was here was waiting to hear how it went, so I couldn't back out now. Of course there were a million forms to fill out and sign, which is so fun when the pen keeps slipping out of your sweaty fingers. *For Pete's sake, get a grip!* I scolded myself. *This is no big deal. You're going to tell her your life story, and she's going to tell you to quit complaining. You have had it so much better than so many other people. What a whiner you are.* It was always great to have my mother in my head at times like these. It was her voice that was always berating me. If I didn't feel badly enough already, she started in. Fortunately, Mom was interrupted.

"Samantha," a woman's voice said just loudly enough to pull me out of my revelry. "I'm Marguerite DeWitt. Please call me Maggie." I was surprised by how young she looked. I guess I was expecting someone who looked like Sarah's granny. I thought all wise women had to be really old—way older than my mom because she had not yet achieved "wise woman" status.

"Come on in," she said, waving me toward the door. It was a cute little office. It was more like a living room than an office. There was no desk for her to sit behind and look down on me as I had imagined. We both plopped down in the overstuffed chairs like two old friends. I was really surprised how at home I felt. "So, what brings you?" she asked.

The panic I had felt initially was starting to recede. "Well, a lot of things I guess. Mostly, I'm getting way too close to 30, and I thought by this time in my life I'd be married with kids. I guess I'm just at loose ends. I don't seem to know what I want or how to begin finding out. My roommate suggested therapy, because I get so emotional when I deal with my family. I'm either devastated by them or so angry I want to chew glass and spit it at them. Unfortunately, a lot of my friends and co-workers seemed to agree with her. My mother, of course, just thinks I should I get a makeover or go to church, and that would solve all my problems. Good ol' Mom, I can always count on her to make me feel like crap. She's always telling me that I am just too sensitive."

"But, why now? Has something changed dramatically for you recently?" Maggie asked. "I imagine your mother has been doing and saying these same things for years."

She seemed to be looking for something, and I wasn't sure I could help her. I don't think I knew the answer to 'Why now?' I spoke slowly, "If I have to give one answer, I think it's the whole 'turning 30' thing. It seems like I just woke up one morning and was closing in on being 30 years old. It just sort of 'happened,' and I keep asking myself, 'Where has my life gone?' I guess I feel totally lost, and I need help finding out who I am. I just can't believe that I'm this old and don't really have anything to show for myself. I think that is what makes me feel out of control with my emotions. I am just so frustrated that life isn't turning out how it was supposed to turn out. You know, like in the fairy tales—where is the flipping knight on the white horse? He's long overdue as far as I'm concerned. And I'm just pissed about it."

"I think I can help you sort some of this out." Maggie smiled. "You do know that your insurance only pays for six sessions, don't you? Fortunately, I have a lot of clients with your insurance, and I have tailored a program just for people in your circumstances. Of course, if you need more sessions, we can try to work something out. Well, we have a lot of work to do, and we need to do it quickly."

Maggie was clearly ready to move forward. "I tell all my clients that I am as much a teacher as I am a therapist. You need to learn new skills and that means you are going to have to be practicing those skills between each session. I'll help you as much as I can, but the hard work is up to you. If you come here for an hour a week and do nothing in between—nothing will happen. If you do your work in between—it could change your life. It's all up to you."

"Well, I'm ready to start." I smiled, but I heard my voice quavering.

"So tell me a little bit about your family, Samantha."

"You can call me Sammy. Everybody does. I was supposed to be a boy because they already had the girl. I don't think they ever really adjusted. They really had the perfect family when they got my brother. My sister is the first and the favorite because she was first; my brother is the baby and the favorite because he's a boy and the baby—and then there is me, sandwiched in the middle just trying to be somebody's favorite for any reason and always failing miserably."

I was on a roll. Dr. DeWitt looked interested, and so I kept going. "I really think my family is pretty average—you know, normal. My mom, Susan, is a really nice person. Everybody loves her—well, except maybe Grandma. The two of them don't get along very well. Everybody else loves her. She's really active in our church and is on a bunch of committees. Dad, his name is Tom, is really nice, too. He's equally involved with the church. Always has been. Mom gripes about his drinking, but he's never mean when he drinks.

He has always stopped at the bar down the street on his way home from work. That was just part of our lives—wait until Dad gets home before we could have dinner, things like that."

"My mom worked for a while when they first got married, but since she was pregnant when they got married, she didn't work very long. I think that may be why she and Grandma have issues. Grandma was pregnant with my mom when she got married, and I think it hacked her off that my mom would make the same mistake. Grandma and Grandpa seemed to hate each other when he was alive, but then he died and now all of a sudden he's a saint. Go figure. Anyway, what else do you want to know?"

"Well, Samantha, I'd like to know how you feel telling me all this? That was a lot of information."

She seemed to have forgotten about the 'call me Sammy' thing, but I decided to ignore it. "What do you mean, how do I feel? I feel fine. You wanted to hear about my family. There they are. Well, I didn't talk about my dad's parents, but we don't see them that often so they didn't seem relevant. How do I feel? I guess I'd have to think about that." I wasn't expecting the throaty laugh that came next.

"Samantha, you can't 'think about' what you are feeling. It doesn't work that way. If you are feeling something, usually you experience it first in your body. Pay attention to your body, particularly your chest, gut, shoulders, and head. Do you feel any tightness or constriction in any of these areas of your body? Start with the sensation that you feel. That sensation may be the indicator that you are experiencing a feeling. Part of therapy is learning about yourself. If you are like most people, by now you have learned to 'stuff' your feelings so that you don't have to deal with them. You probably only 'feel' when things have gotten so bad that you are unable to control yourself, am I right? Does that seem to fit your experience of yourself?"

All I could think about was falling apart with Sarah when my mom had 'done her thing' on me a few months ago. "Yes, it fits. I just can't stop crying some times. Or, I get so angry that I'm yelling, throwing things, and stomping around the apartment. I just seem to be overreacting to things more lately."

"Unfortunately, what you do is 'stuff' until you can't control your emotions and then you 'burst.' That outburst seems excessive to you, and then you feel bad about doing it. It may surprise you, but you really don't have to live like that. You can actually react appropriately, in the moment, when things happen. When you learn to express your feelings appropriately in the moment, there are way fewer overreactions. We're all human so none of us can do life perfectly, just think of it as you'll be more in control." Maggie was very patient and extremely empathetic. "What you are experiencing is not that unusual, especially for women. We're taught that if we cry, we're weak, and if we're angry, we're bitches. It's hard to find the middle ground. But, that's why you are here."

"Now, let's try again," Maggie continued. "You just told me that most likely your dad is an alcoholic and your mother is really angry and appears to take her anger out on you. How does that make you feel?"

Not good! I felt like someone had just punched me in the gut. I am not sure if I made a noise or not, but I felt like all the air had left my body. *I didn't say those things. I wouldn't say those things about my family.* All I could think of to say was, "That's not what I said." I just sat there looking at this woman like she was crazy. *Where could she have gotten those crazy ideas about my family?* I noticed that tears were stinging my eyes. I repeated myself, "I didn't say that."

"Okay, Samantha, you didn't say that, I did. When you were telling me about yourself, essentially that is what you said. Have you never thought about your dad as an alcoholic?" I could hear the tenderness in her voice and knew that she wasn't saying this to be mean, but the honest answer was 'No.' I had never even thought about it.

"I have never really thought about it like that," I answered. "I guess I thought alcoholics were the homeless people living on the streets and eating out of dumpsters. My dad is a sweet guy. He's not mean. He's not anything really. He's quiet. He just comes home, eats, watches TV or reads the paper, and goes to bed. I do have to admit that I rarely see him without a drink in his hand."

"So he doesn't really interact with others in the family? He's kind of in his own world? He's home, but he's not really there for you to bounce ideas off of or to just talk with? Does that sort of sum him up?" Maggie asked.

"Well, yes. That's the way he's always been. He works hard at his job, but that's all he does. I guess that's why my mom gets so angry at him, because she feels that she does it all. She took care of us kids by herself, really. She was the one at the school functions like plays and ball games. Whatever we were involved in doing, she was there. They never fight. I don't think she ever tells him she's mad. She just doesn't speak to him—God, sometimes for weeks on end. I hate to say it, but I think he likes it. Then she's not on his back. Mostly, she just criticizes him when she does talk to him."

"You know," I continued, "I had friends whose parents were alcoholics; my dad wasn't like what they described. I'm not so sure that he really falls into that category." Even as I said the words, I doubted myself. This felt too right.

"When you tell me that your father stopped every night for a drink before he came home, I have to at least suspect alcoholism. Most people don't need a drink every night. I assume that he and your mother also drank at home, so it wasn't just one drink. Am I right?"

"Yes. Alcohol is just part of life in our family. In fact, on some weekends it's not unusual for my dad to make Bloody Marys, especially if someone comes over to the house on a Saturday or Sunday morning. I just never see him really drunk—well a few times, I guess, but doesn't everybody get drunk a few times?"

It seemed like there was a giant puzzle out there—called my life—and I was starting to see some of the pieces fitting together.

"Samantha, I'm going to give you some ideas for books to read on something called 'codependence.' It is a name for people who have grown up in homes where addiction is present. I'm also going to teach you a model that I have developed while working with women. It will help you to understand yourself a little better, and hopefully, it will help you to learn the skills you need to deal with your family a little more effectively. And, we're going to focus on recognizing feelings. You may actually begin to get your needs met in your relationships both with your family and possibly significant others in your life. How does that sound?"

"Are you kidding? It sounds great!" I actually felt hopeful. I could see how not being so dependent upon others and their opinions of me might feel like I was more in control of my life. This felt really good.

"Samantha," Maggie continued, "this is going to be the hardest thing you have ever done. People don't like it when you change. Your relationships have a pattern, a flow. Right now, everybody kind of knows what they can do or say and how other family members will handle the things they say and do. If you change that 'status quo,' it is going to throw a monkey wrench into a lot of people's lives. They won't like it, and they will blame you—rightfully so. You will be the one who is changing. I also want to reassure you that it will be the best thing you have ever done for yourself. You will be free to be the person you are and who you were born to be. I just want to be clear that it isn't easy and will often be painful. Still game to try?"

"Yes, I am!" I was ecstatic. This all sounded great, even with the disclaimer about my family—I can hear between the lines—not being very happy about me trying to better myself.

"I'm excited for you," Maggie responded. "I always tell people, 'You never know what you are saying *yes* to, until you try it.' I'll be interested to hear how your week goes. Keep paying attention to your body. Keep some sort of journal to make you focus when you experience a feeling—just pick up any spiral notebook—you don't need anything fancy. Try to keep your writing simple. Start with, I feel... and then fill in the blank. Think basic emotions like happy, sad, angry, and scared. When you notice the sensations in your body, you are probably experiencing one of those feelings. You just need to put the name on the feeling that corresponds with the sensation in your body. I'll talk more about journaling in the next session. Start simple for now."

"The second thing I want you to do is to journal about that voice you hear in your head. I heard you say something about your mom's voice in your head and when you hear her in your head, you feel bad. I want you to start recognizing that voice when it occurs and to write down what you hear. You might also want to write down the feelings that come up for you when you hear the voice. You may be surprised that you have more than Mom living in your head. Please try to do the journaling every day. If something happens that upsets you, it is best to write about it immediately. Carry a little notebook in your purse. If you can't do that, write about the event that night after supper—not at bedtime or you won't sleep well."

"The last thing I want you to do is to think about your breathing. It sounds silly I know, but my hunch is that you spend a lot of your time doing fight or flight breathing. That means shallow breathing. I'll talk more about it next week, but for now just focus on your breathing before you go to sleep. Breathe in to the count of four, through your nose, and then out to the count of four through your mouth. If you keep your hand on your belly as you do this, you should feel your belly rise and fall. If you don't, breathe deeper until you do. Do this slowly over and over until you feel yourself begin to relax. You might also want to practice breathing like this at the office when you are feeling particularly stressed."

"I know I've given you a lot to think about and do. I hope I'm not overwhelming you. It is going to be hard, but it is worth all the hard work because you are worth it. You deserve to have your own life and be your own person. Your feelings are the pathway to finding yourself. Do you have any questions?"

I couldn't think of a thing to say. I just shook my head with a grin spreading from ear to ear. I must have looked like an idiot.

"Make an appointment with my office manager, and I'll see you next week, okay? Here's my card if you have any questions or problems. It was good to meet you, Samantha. Take care."

I walked out of her office like I was on Cloud Nine. What a kick! I liked this person. She was bright, funny and just plain nice. I could do this. I couldn't wait to tell Sarah how it had gone.

I made an appointment with the office manager for the same time next week and headed back to work. I felt better just talking about things with someone besides Sarah. I also felt better because I had a serious suspicion that there really was a light at the end of the tunnel.

chapter 3

"I'M HOME! ARE you here? Sarah, where are you?" I was all over the apartment with Shiloh at my heels. "Yes, I see you. I'm sorry if I didn't pay any attention to you when I walked in." A quick pat and a rub of her belly, and Shiloh was off sniffing for food in the couch. She was always sure to come up with something when she buried her nose in the couch cushions. Neither Sarah nor I are the best housekeepers in the world—much to my mother's chagrin. Shiloh loved us for that reason alone. She was our vacuum and our mop. It worked out for all concerned, well—except for my mother.

Sarah came walking out of her bathroom with her hair in a towel. "What's up?" She was smiling. She had to know by the look on my face that things had gone well.

"It was amazing! I'm so excited! Dr. DeWitt told me about some books to read, and she wants me to keep a journal about feelings. Oh my God! I feel so happy! I'm actually hopeful that maybe things might change. This one is going to shock you—she said she thinks my dad might be an alcoholic."

"Might be," Sarah literally chirped. "Might be! Oh, Sammy, are you kidding me that you really didn't know? I've known since about the first week after I met your family. Nobody talked about it, so I didn't either. It never dawned on me that you actually didn't know. I just thought that you didn't want to talk about it. Well, as they say, 'Denial isn't just a river in Egypt.'"

"I just never thought about it that way. I know he drinks. I know the whole family drinks, but to think of any of them as alcoholics is just too much. It makes me wonder about a lot of stuff now. It's funny how just saying something like that out loud brings you up short—like snap! Wow! I'm blown away. She said so much about how our family did stuff, and she was right on. It has really made me think. She gave me great ideas for learning how to get in touch with feelings. She was also pretty careful about telling me it won't be easy. But hey, what is? Dealing with my mother is difficult in the best of circumstances. How bad can it get?"

Never say those words out loud when you are dealing with my family. I seem to have to learn everything the hard way. Like an idiot I picked up the phone when it rang without looking at caller ID.

"Brian's birthday is today. Are you coming for the party tonight or are you too busy for us?" These kinds of questions were never really questions with my mother. They were demands, but she always pretended they were questions. So, I acted like this was one, too.

"Sure Mom, I wouldn't miss it. Actually, you've never let me forget the one year I did miss, so I'm smart enough not to repeat that." I broke my arm in a volleyball game and missed Brian's party three years ago. You would have thought that I did it on purpose. Of course, Sarah only makes it worse by telling me that I probably *did* do it on purpose. *Nobody's that sick, are they?*

"Well," she continued without a pause, therefore not hearing a word I said. "We are so excited about his gift that I just can't wait for you to see it."

"What is it, Mom—a Madonna CD like you got for me?" I hate Madonna so her gift couldn't have been worse. Well, wait a minute—when she buys me clothes, size 'small,' when I haven't seen size 'small' since birth, that really frosts my cookies, too. My mom seems to have an uncanny ability to buy things that really piss me off. Maybe she tries, but to me it looks like she researches the stuff I hate and then buys it. Oh well, maybe it's just the older generation being out of touch with young people, yeah right!

"We bought him a car! I'm so excited. I just can't wait for him to see it!" My mom was squealing like a pig. I could hear how excited she was, but I felt like a bomb had just exploded in my head.

"A car, you bought him a car, a real car? Are you kidding me, Mom? Because, this isn't funny." I went totally numb, kind of dead, cold. I actually felt a prickly sensation in my scalp. This could not be true!

"Oh, Sammy, you have always been so jealous of your brother. You know how far he has to drive to work, and the gas prices are killing him. We got him a Prius so he would get better gas mileage. Can't you just be happy for him? Just come over later for the party. You'll see it then. Don't you tell him and spoil the surprise." She was still squealing as she hung up.

"Oh, my God! Oh, my God! I just can't flippin believe it!" I found myself stomping around my apartment. Even Shiloh ran for cover. I think I was yelling. I know I felt like I was going to explode.

"What is it? What's wrong?" Sarah came running from her bedroom where she always goes when I get a call from my family. I used to think it was because she was polite. I'm starting to wonder if she's really running for cover like the dog. Knowing my family, there is always the chance that there will be blood and guts somewhere.

"I can't believe it. They are giving him a car for his birthday—a Prius." I was still stomping, still yelling. "They haven't given me anything, ever! What is it with them? What am I, chopped liver? If I act like I'm upset, she tells me that I'm jealous of Brian. Well, maybe I am. What do I have to do to be treated like him—or like Kay for that matter? They are such assholes. Do they do this stuff on purpose? Are they trying to make me feel like shit? Are they really clueless about how much this hurts me?"

"Okay, this seems like a good time to start that journal you were just telling me about," Sarah said calmly. A little too calmly I think. I am pretty sure Sarah was trying to get me to focus on something that would stop me from the yelling and stomping. It wouldn't be the first time we'd gotten a call from the landlord about noise. My family tended to turn me into a raving lunatic.

"You are so right. I'm writing all this shit down. I can't wait to tell Maggie DeWitt about this." I stomped into my room. I dragged my chair up to the desk while throwing the book I'd bought to use as a journal onto the desk. "Fuck them! Fuck all of them!"

I did start writing, and I couldn't believe all the old memories that came tumbling out of my head. My God, where had I kept these memories filed? I hadn't thought of a lot of them in years. There were so many recollections of Kay and Brian getting things I wanted. Kay always got the new clothes. I always got the hand-me-down clothes when Kay was finished with them. Brian got new things because he was a boy. There were things I remember wanting, asking for, and then watching at the next holiday as Kay opened that particular gift. *Could that happen by accident? Wow! There were an awful lot of examples for them to all be accidents.* I also remembered asking for a loan only to be told that if I couldn't afford something, I shouldn't be buying it. Yet, here was a blatant example of one of the other kids getting something that I would never have been given. I would have been told to earn the money for it if I wanted it. *What was up with this crap? What was up with these people?*

I probably wrote and cried for well over an hour. When I quit writing—and crying—I felt much better. Sarah had gone out with friends, squeezing my shoulder as she left. She was always invited to gatherings at my house, but she always had other plans—smart girl. I jumped in the shower so I wouldn't miss the cake. I realized I had already missed dinner. I knew I'd never hear the end of this. *Oh well, me missing dinner isn't the thing Mom will be upset about tomorrow—she's getting a piece of my mind!*

Everyone stopped talking and just looked at me when I walked through the door. Great! It's always nice to make an inconspicuous entrance. "What?" I said to all of them, and yet to no one in particular—ready to fight. My mother gave me the 'evil eye.' She's been giving me this same look as long as I can remember, and my resolve to confront her went right out the window. *Shit!*

"Well, I thought you'd never get here. We've been waiting all night. We couldn't do anything until you got here. You just can't be on time, can you? Would it have killed you to have called to say that you weren't coming for dinner? I swear, Samantha, it's like you try to hurt me. Kay and Brian don't treat me like this." She looked around at everyone in the room as if she was expecting all of them to give her some sort of award for service beyond the call of duty for putting up with me.

Grandma piped up from her place on the couch—well, more 'in' the couch. She seems to have grown smaller as I've grown older, and I swear the couch almost swallows her. "Leave her alone, Susan. She's here now. Let's have the cake and let Brian open his presents. You've been making such a big deal out of this, it better be good."

"Oh, Mother, just be quiet." My mom didn't like to be told what to do by anyone, least of all my grandma. "I'm going to get the cake. Somebody grab a camera so we can get Brian's picture." Mom was chirping again. Of course, the focus was now on Brian, so she was all sweetness and light.

I pulled up a chair and sat at the dining room table. Brian punched my arm, which was his way of saying 'Hello.' We have quaint little ways of communicating—I'll have a black and blue spot for a week. Kay and Mike were across the table. The kids were off somewhere. I could hear them but not see them. I heard my mom yelling for everyone to get to the dining room to sing "Happy Birthday." *Oh yeah, this was just great—home sweet home.* I noticed Dad was watching the television in his chair next to the couch, and neither he nor Grandma moved toward the table. I also noticed that both of them had a beer in their hand. *Hmmm.*

Mom came out carrying the cake, and we all sang. Of course we devoured our cake and then moved on to the 'event' we had all been waiting for—the opening of the gift. Mom blindfolded Brian and all of us dutifully followed as she pushed him toward the garage.

"What the hell are you doing, Ma?" I could hear that Brian was pissed off. He didn't much like being pushed around by anyone, and this behavior was really out of character for Mom.

"Oh shush, you big lug!" She opened the garage door and took off the blindfold, and handed him a set of keys. I thought his eyes were going to bug out of his head.

"Oh, my God, Ma! You got me a Prius! This is great! The guys will never believe it! Where are the keys? I'm going to take it over to show Amanda." The way mom reacted, you would have thought that he had just announced he was going to kill somebody.

"Brian, you can't leave now! Look what we did for you. Everyone is here just to see you!" Mom was begging. A flash bulb seemed to go off in my head—she was trying to buy him back from the current girlfriend. I could have saved her a lot of money—most of his relationships lasted about three months, and then they were over. *Wow! Another flash—that sounds suspiciously like my relationships. Hmmm.*

"Let him go, Susan." Grandma had pulled herself out of the couch and followed us to the garage. If it pissed Mom off, Grandma was for it. She pulled on Mom while

Mom pulled on Brian. Of course, Brian was stronger, so he pulled away and headed for the car. Grandma pulled Mom back to the kitchen.

"Nice thank you," I muttered under my breath on my way back in for another piece of cake. No matter how many problems I had with my mom, nobody could bake like she could. I wasn't missing out on seconds.

"What did you say?" Mom asked. She was angry, and she had just found her target.

"I just said, 'Nice thank you.' Seems to me like if someone gave me a car, I'd muster up a thank you before I headed off to show all my friends." I heard the sarcasm in my voice and knew that it wasn't lost on my mom but didn't really care at this point.

"Well, that's the difference between you and Brian, Sammy." Mom was practically snarling at me. "Brian says 'thank you' to me all the time in the things he does for me. You are always too busy for the family. We are always a bother to you. What have you ever done for me? You can't even remember what I want for my birthday." Mom was clearly moving into her rant mode. This was going down the toilet fast.

"Mom, I asked you what you wanted, and you said you didn't want to make any decisions about that. How was I supposed to remember something you had mentioned weeks prior?" I felt trapped, and I was fighting to find a way out. With my mom, fighting back is like being blindfolded and swinging at a piñata—you just keep swinging the stick, never hitting anything, and never getting the prize.

"That's what I mean," she continued. "No one is as important as you are. You don't pay attention because you don't care. For God's sake, are you eating more cake? You are going to be as big as a house if you don't stop eating so much. You aren't like Kay. She can eat anything without gaining a pound, but then she is so busy, she burns it off."

"So if Kay's busy, that's a good thing, but if I'm busy, I'm self-centered. Okay, that's it. I'm out of here!" I ran out of the house hearing the door slam behind me. I ran like someone was after me. In a way, I felt like they were. *What is wrong with me? I don't fit in with these people. They all hate me.*

Again, like a video tape replay, I cried all the way home with Lizzie doing most of the work navigating herself. She was probably just happy to be away from the new car scent of Brian's new Prius. At least I got my second piece of cake. God, can my mother bake! Nobody makes butter cream frosting like my mother. This is clearly a love-hate relationship. Unfortunately, the love part revolves solely around food.

My cell phone rang just as I reached my parking lot. "Sam, why do you always have to be such a drama queen?" My sister's voice stung even through the phone.

"Kay, please, just leave me alone for a while. I'm trying to figure this all out. It doesn't help when you just side with Mom and make me out to be the bad guy."

"Samantha, it is just not as bad as you make it out to be. You're the one who creates the problems. If you would just go along with her, everything would be fine."

"Kay, I'm not you. For you things are fine. They don't treat me the way they treat you. Mom, especially, is nice to you. She's not nice to me. Can't you see how differently she treats me? Am I crazy? Am I the only one who can see this?"

"Well, I don't think you are crazy, but you certainly exaggerate everything. You always have."

Why did I feel like I was talking to Mom again? "Kay, I have to go. I'll talk to you later."

Sarah was already home and in her bedroom when I let myself in the apartment. Tim was with her. I could hear them talking. *Geez, this was getting to be a habit. He has been here every weekend lately. I wonder if this is starting to get really serious? I like Tim. He is a really nice guy and obviously in love with Sarah.* In the past Sarah has been the holdout. There have been a lot of guys in love with her, but she's always said that she was going to be "choosy." I wondered if she was getting close to "choosing" Tim. I wouldn't blame her. He's really cute, smart, and successful. *Oh well, I can talk to her about the 'disaster' tomorrow.*

As Shiloh and I snuggled, I wondered if I would ever get to sleep with all the crap swirling in my head from the family experience. *A car—how amazing is that when they won't give me the time of day? Some things never change—especially my mother where my brother is concerned.*

I remembered the breathing technique Dr. DeWitt had talked about, the "counting to four" thing. Lying there with the dog, I began to breathe deeply. *How'd that go? Breathe in through my nose, 1 – 2 – 3 – 4, then breathe out through my mouth, 1 – 2 – 3 – 4.* I did it a few times and could feel myself beginning to relax. *Hey, I'll have to tell her that this works.* Shiloh was out before I could do it once the whole way through. I never thought I'd get to sleep but using the deep breathing techniques, I was finally able let go of the day's events. Maybe Shiloh's snoring helped, too.

chapter 4

"Wow, you've had quite a week, Samantha," Dr. DeWitt responded after I dumped my litany of events on her. Maggie, as she had asked me to call her, seemed pleased with my attempts at journaling and with the fact that I had used the breathing techniques. I really liked how she listened. Sarah was the only one who had ever really listened to me in the past. It just felt good to be me and not to be judged.

"I know it feels better just to talk about these problems, Samantha. The problem is that just talking about them doesn't change anything. You need to learn some new coping skills if you are ever going to feel good about yourself after these encounters with your family. I told you last week that I was going to teach you a model for understanding yourself and your behavior. I think now is a good time to begin. I'll use the events that you just related to me to help make the model clearer. If you have any questions, just stop me."

Maggie had one whole wall of white board. She stood up and started drawing. "Sometimes, it is true that a picture is worth a thousand words," she laughed as drew a stick figure on the board. "I wasn't an art major, so you just have to use your imagination."

"The goal of therapy is for a person to be a healthy, boundaried adult *most* of the time." Maggie had drawn a line in an arc over a stick figure. It looked like a stick person in an upside down glass. Over the top of the boundary she wrote the words, 'I Am—I Know Me.' "Living in the moment, being a person of integrity—saying what you mean and meaning what you say, being authentic or real, are the hallmarks of a healthy adult. That boundary signifies where you stop and the world begins."

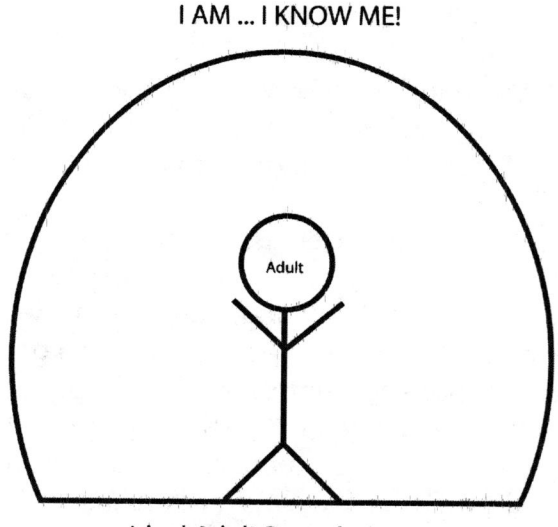

Ideal Adult Boundaries

"No one can remain perfectly boundaried all the time—you'd have to be a perfect person to accomplish that, and we'll leave that to God. So what does a healthy, boundaried adult look and sound like? The healthy adult knows who she is, which means she knows what she feels, what she needs, and is able to express those feelings and needs appropriately. She is also able to listen to other people's feelings and needs and to validate their feelings and needs as equal to her own. Finally, the healthy adult is able to negotiate so that she gets her needs met." Maggie had been writing these key points as she talked. "Are you with me so far? I know it's a lot to digest so I'll give you a handout to help you remember everything I'm saying." (The handout Maggie gave Samantha is in Appendix 1.)

"This sounds really good. I can't imagine getting my needs met with my family, but it's a great idea." I was intrigued, but also confused at the same time. "How do you actually *do* it?"

"Well," Maggie continued, "it's not as easy as it sounds. Let's just continue to look at you and what happens when you're with your family. Remember, I said no one is perfect? Well, because we are all ordinary human beings this boundary has holes in it—the holes are what make us unique. In other words, the holes in my boundary are different than the holes in your boundary, and your friend Sarah has different ones from either you or me. Our unique environments make us vulnerable to different things—those old traumatic events create our issues of today." As she talked, she erased parts of the boundary she had drawn earlier.

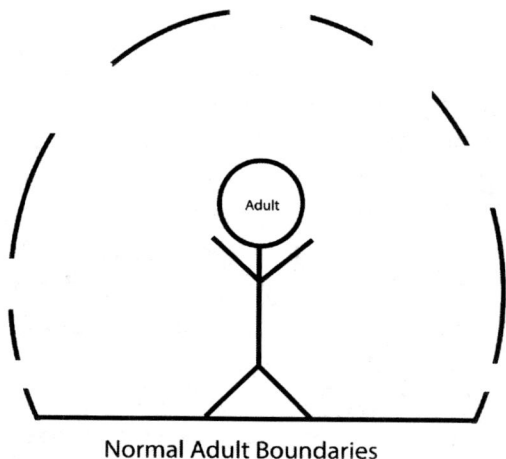

Normal Adult Boundaries

"The holes also change in relation to everyday stressors, physical issues like sickness, or experiencing PMS. Let me give you an example. My father was a rager. I have a hole in my boundary for loud, angry men—a hole created in my family-of-origin. So when a man speaks very loudly, I have to remind myself to breathe so that I don't overreact to that behavior. I have that hole just because I was raised in a family where raging was the norm—so the past rears its ugly head in my present when someone yells. Does that make sense so far, Samantha?"

"Yes, if I understand you correctly, things from my past have created holes in my boundary. You are going to teach me to react differently when someone hits one of those holes, right?" I felt like Eliza Doolittle. I wanted to yell, "I've got it! By George, I've got it!"

"That's exactly right, Samantha. And, there is also another element in this phenomenon. The holes are created in our family-of-origin, but current stressors and physical factors make those holes bigger or smaller. You will do better getting 'grounded', staying adult, when you are feeling well physically. On the other hand, if you have a cold, if you haven't had enough sleep because you are overworked, if you are experiencing PMS, or slightly depressed, these things influence your ability to stay boundaried if someone attacks you. So, getting back to my example, if I'm feeling well and not stressed, I will be able to confront the man who is speaking loudly and ask him to lower his voice. If I'm not in a good place, I won't be able to handle it as well."

"When someone says or does something that gets inside the boundary, that is called a 'trigger'. It is a psychological attack. They have hit one of the holes from an old issue, or you just have bigger holes because it's a bad time for you. When you are triggered, you will feel it in your body. Perhaps it will feel like a punch in the gut; perhaps you'll feel your shoulders tighten; perhaps you will feel your chest constrict; or you may get a raging headache. Your body knows when you are under attack. When we feel attacked and can't support ourselves enough to fight back, then we regress, get little, and feel threatened and afraid. The adult part of us sort of 'fades' and the Regressed (R) part takes over the interaction with the other person."

Maggie drew a little person inside the boundary as she talked. She also partially erased the 'adult' figure under the glass. "This phenomenon usually only happens in relations with others so I'm drawing another person outside the boundary." She added.

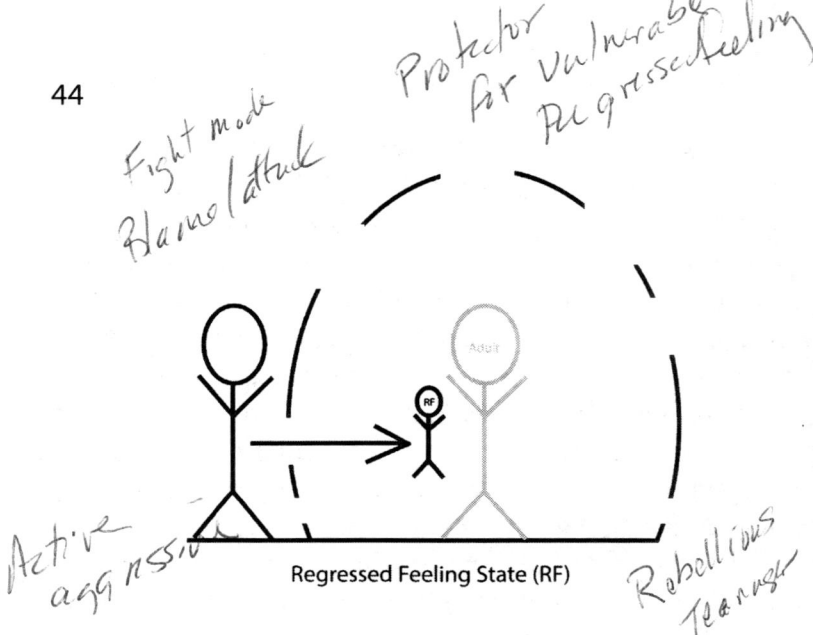

Regressed Feeling State (RF)

Trying to sound somewhat psychologically sophisticated, I said, "It sounds like you are talking about the inner child?"

"Not exactly, Samantha. There really isn't an inner child, even though it feels like that sometimes. When an event happens that reminds us of another time and place, we sort of 'flash back' to that time, frequently it's because it happened when we were children. We re-experience the feelings we had at that time—it feels like we are that child again. The reason for that is because when we are little, we really do experience things as life and death issues—black and white. If a child is lost, he or she doesn't have the cognitive ability to say, 'This is temporary—Mom or Dad will find me soon.' The child naturally feels scared to death. We freeze-frame those kinds of events and file them so that if something like that happens again, we know what to do."

"You mean the way all those things started to come up when I was journaling? I couldn't believe how stuff just kept popping up that I hadn't thought about in years. I guess I really do have a filing cabinet in my head." I certainly could understand what Maggie was saying about arousing old feelings from the past.

"That's exactly what I am talking about," she replied. "The gift of a car triggered all those old memories of times when you felt you were treated unfairly as a child. I know this is a lot of information, Samantha, but you seem to be staying with me, so I'm going to continue. We learn to protect ourselves very early. Have you heard of the fight, flight, or freeze response?" Maggie asked.

"Well, I had an introductory psych class when I was in college. I don't remember much about it." I felt a little ashamed to admit that I hadn't paid attention when obviously it would have helped if I had.

"That's okay, I'll just go over some of the key concepts again for you, but this time I'm going to add a twist. I've added some character to those very ordinary, normal reactions. I see them as sub-personalities or 'the little people' who take on a life of their own in the service of protecting us. These reactions are hardwired into our brains so that we can survive in this dog-eat-dog world. First, let's look at the fight reaction. When you got the information about Brian's car, you reacted. You went into fight mode. You were yelling and stomping around; you were angry. You were swearing and essentially throwing a temper tantrum—not always a bad thing, by the way." Maggie laughed in a mysterious sort of way.

"Whenever you hear yourself swearing, especially saying 'Fuck you,' you are in this fight response. I call this sub-personality the 'Rebellious Teenager (RT),' because that's the way she looks and sounds. She is a protector for that vulnerable regressed part. The problem is that she goes overboard. She is a little *too* aggressive, *too* blaming, *too* attacking, and *too* threatening. She can be pretty scary. Just so you know, it has nothing to do with being a teenager. This part shows up at around age two. Children at this age are said to be in the 'terrible twos,' because that is when toddlers decide they are different than the others around them. Their favorite word is "No." I only call it a teenager because this part is very verbal."

"Oh, I remember when my nieces went through that phase." I started to laugh. "I remember a time when my niece was playing with a toy. She would pull the string and the toy would say, 'Can you find the clock?' and she would start screaming at it—'No! No! No!' She had to be about two years old. She would never let anyone do anything for her."

"That's it!" Maggie said. "That's exactly what I'm talking about, except that we are now in adult bodies and that behavior is inappropriate."

Rebellious Teenager (RT)

Maggie drew the "fighter" inside the boundary. "I'm drawing an arrow from the teenager to the 'other' character because the teenager's focus is always on the other—never on herself. In her mind, the 'other' is the problem."

"Intuitively Sarah knew you needed to focus on yourself and your feelings. That is probably why she encouraged you to journal. I think she was afraid you would punch a hole in the wall, or do something equally destructive. It's never okay to hurt people or things with your anger—especially yourself. I had a client who broke her hand putting it through a wall. The fight part is very powerful. It is this sub-personality that has taken over when your anger feels out of control. We'll talk more about this part in later sessions. Do you have any questions about the fight response?" Maggie asked.

"No, unfortunately, I think I understand that part perfectly." I was feeling a little uncomfortable because I seemed to fit this part to a tee. "Do you have any nicer parts for me to identify with?"

Maggie laughed, "You're funny. There are no bad parts, Samantha. We all have all the parts I'm describing. We just all have a different default part—the part that we go to automatically, before we have time to think. You seem to go first to the fight part when you are triggered by your family, so I started it with it."

"The second type of reaction I'm going to describe is the flight part. If you tease a dog, it will bite your hand (the fight reaction), or it will run away (the flight reaction.) Because we are socialized not to just run away from people, we run psychologically. Although when you walked out on your family, you did actually use the flight response as any other animal uses it. Typically, though, we just shut down and shut up. I heard you say that you had done that a few times during the course of the evening with your parents. This is the same angry, blaming energy that we saw in that fight response; it's just that this response is quiet. No one knows what is going on with you. I call this sub-personality the 'Silent Rebellious Teenager (SRT).' She has the same energy as her sister, the Rebellious Teenager; it is just a different, quieter expression of the energy."

Flight
shut down / shut up

Passive aggressive

Silent Rebellious Teenager (SRT)

Maggie drew the second teenager under the boundary. The arrow was again pointing outward toward the 'other' person, this time the line was broken.

"Let's use your mom as an example. When your mom is being quiet, have you ever asked her, "What's wrong?"

"Of course, I have. She always says, 'Nothing.'"

Maggie leaned forward. "Samantha, when she says 'nothing' do you believe her?"

"No," I exclaimed. "She gets this look on her face that tells me she could just kill me. I know she is furious, but she keeps saying 'Nothing's wrong.' How do I fight that? I always feel like I can't win and basically give up. Wow, you really nailed it. This is exactly how my mom acts."

"It is hard to win in these situations. This is a classic double message and ultimately a double bind. Often, you really can't win, and it is better not to try. That is why I drew a broken line rather than a direct one. There is no such thing as direct communication with this sub-personality."

Maggie looked at me quizzically. "What's going on?"

A light bulb seemed to go off in my head. "Wait! I do the same thing sometimes. I get it! How funny is this? I can see myself *and* other people in this model. Maggie, it's amazing how simple it is, yet I can also see how hard it will be to make it work because it's so much a part of me. I didn't even realize that I did it until right this moment."

"You're right. It will be hard. But, being aware of your automatic responses will help you in all sorts of situations, Samantha. The flight part is not active-aggressive like the fight part. It is passive-aggressive. I'll give you a paper I wrote to help people deal with the passive-aggressive people in their lives. (The handout Maggie gave to Samantha on passive-aggressive behavior is in Appendix II.) The flight part is angry, like the fight part, but is more afraid of conflict. This Silent Rebellious Teenager won't say anything in a straightforward way about the anger. The anger from this part shows up in digs, sarcasm, cruel jokes and lots of other sly ways that I outline more thoroughly in the paper I'm giving you."

Maggie continued, "The thing to remember about both the fight and flight parts is that the focus is on the other person. When we are stuck in either of these parts, we think to ourselves, 'If only this person were different, I'd be fine.' When this happens, we are 'other oriented' and give our power away to other people."

"I imagine that might sound funny to you." Maggie continued. "Most people feel really powerful when they are in that Rebellious Teenager place. You have to keep in mind that this Teenager exhibits 'pseudo power.' To yourself, you look really powerful and scary stomping around while cursing. Sometimes you even actually tell people to their faces where they can go—and it's usually not a nice place." Maggie laughed as she said it. I laughed also because I could certainly identify with the part.

Maggie continued. "This show of strength, however, is not from a place of real power. It is a powerful reaction to the other person. When you are reacting to something or someone, you are not in your power. Only when you are in that boundaried, adult place, can you be "present" to the other person. When you can hear their needs as well as your own—that is real power. Does this make sense to you, Samantha?"

"I think so. I know I feel powerful when I'm throwing things but, when I'm done with my tantrum, I feel guilty. I don't feel good about what I've done and said. So, I guess I understand what you mean about that not being 'real' power. I guess it will get clearer as I work with it."

"You're right, Samantha. It will get clearer as you learn to hear and see the parts as they appear—because they will all appear. It is human nature to have all these parts, which brings me to the next and last reactive response."

"It is the freeze reaction. That would be like the 'deer in the headlights' response. We just freeze and don't know what to do. I heard you say that you felt numb and cold when you first heard about Brian's car. You froze. And what did you do next? I don't know if you remember, but you started to criticize yourself and wonder what was wrong with *you*. That is how we freeze. We create a character, another sub-personality, who becomes our Internal Critic (IC). This part stops us in our tracks—freezes our ability to respond. The Critic has something to say about everything. It knows all the rules and, of course, the rules are all black and white because we learned them so early—before we were capable of abstract thought—gray thinking."

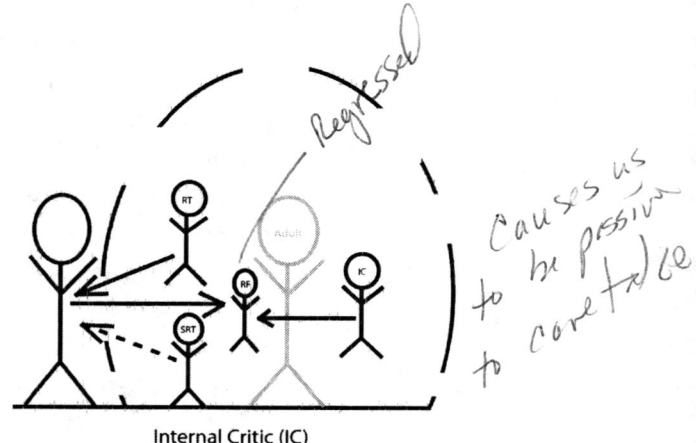

Internal Critic (IC)

Maggie drew the last character, the Internal Critic, under the boundary. This time the arrow pointed at the Regressed part.

"Hey, it's getting really crowded in there! No wonder it's so overwhelming in my head sometimes." It would have probably seemed really funny if it hadn't seemed so right. I could see myself so clearly in these 'characters' that Maggie was drawing.

Maggie continued. "You're right. It does get overwhelming. Just remember that we create this Internal Critic to protect the vulnerable part of us. It protects us differently than the fight or flight parts of us do. The Critic focuses on us, not the other person that's why I drew the arrow pointing inward. The message from within is, 'If only I were different, then he or she will love me.' The Critic causes us to be passive, to care take others, and to always try to please people at the expense of our own needs. Where the fight and flight modes are looking outward, wanting others to be different, the Critic—that freeze mode—is looking inward and telling us to be different, that somehow the problem is our fault."

"Oh, my gosh, Maggie! I do all of these things. I can be both those teenagers and I have a huge critic. How did that happen?"

"The Critic is a conglomerate of all the old voices and rules created by mom, dad, grandparents, church, school, and society as a whole. The Critic has stored all the rules it has ever heard and expects us to be able to do all the things perfectly. For example, the Critic has rules about what kind of a worker you should be, what kind of housekeeper you should be, what kind of daughter, roommate, sister, etc., you should be, and you can never do it all. The Critic will drive you crazy, if you let her. Because of her demands for perfection, we are often so overwhelmed that we are immobilized."

"Remember, no one could do all the things that their Critic thinks they should be able to do. There just aren't enough hours in the day. That's why it is so important to get a handle on how much your Critic talks to you and what she is saying. That is why I asked you to start journaling about that. I know the whole thing about the car came up and took precedence this week, but starting now I want you to pay attention to what you hear in your head as you go about your day."

"Keep the goal in mind at all times—dealing with people from that boundaried, adult state." Maggie erased the lines from the regressed, reactive sub-personalities. "It is the adult's job to interact with other people. The adult needs to talk to each sub-personality, listen to her needs, and then talk to the other person so that those needs are met. I will be repeating this often—It is NEVER okay for the regressed, reactive parts to talk to or interact with others.

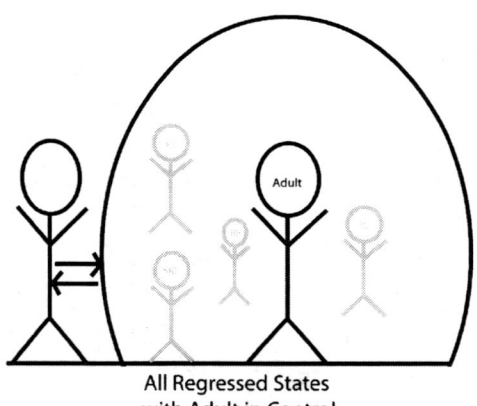

All Regressed States
with Adult in Control

"So, does all this make sense? Have I managed to totally overwhelm you?" Maggie asked with a concerned smile. "It's a lot to dump on you in one session, but I wanted to cover it so that you can begin using it. This will give you lots to think about and work on during the next four sessions. Take a deep breath as you absorb these ideas. That reminds me, I told you at our first meeting that I'd talk more about breathing. Just remember when you are triggered, try to do the breathing exercise I showed you. It worked for you when you were trying to get to sleep; it will work for you when you are triggered. I promise."

It was amazing how good I felt when I took the deep breath Maggie had suggested. "Yes, it makes sense! Are you kidding? I love this! I see each one of my family members in this model and, of course, I see myself. I know you want me to focus on how this can work for me, but part of how it works is to help me see that other people are sometimes stuck in something other than a healthy adult place. I see how I do all of these things. I really have a big Internal Critic. I'll pay attention to that. After our first session, I didn't understand for sure what you meant when you said to write about what I heard the voices saying things in my head, but now I do."

"This is great, Maggie! I think I'm going to try to get a mental picture of where people are if they aren't acting like healthy adults. That might help me to talk to them differently—maybe even get my needs met. This stuff happens at work all the time too. My office is mostly women, and we do have our 'PMS moments.' I'll journal and we'll talk about it next week." I was thrilled and motivated. I could see how this could change things—especially me.

"It sounds like you are beginning to understand these important tools, Samantha! I've presented the model with you under the glass—the one with a boundary. You need to see everyone in your environment as a person who has some version of a healthy, or not so healthy, boundary—everyone is 'a person under glass.'" We both laughed at that visual.

"The most important thing I want you to take away from our session today is that how people behave is *not* about you. When I first put this model up, I drew that boundary, the upside down glass, around the person. When I erased parts of the boundary, the holes had to do with family of origin issues, etc. When your parents, friends, or co-workers *react* to you, it's *not* about you. It is about their own issues or current stressors and their defensive reactions. If your mom is angry, she has a responsibility to tell you what she is angry about. It is not your job to guess or to figure it out—you'll never be able to do it. Do you see why now? Because it is *her* issue—it is a hole in *her* glass." Maggie continued, "If you have a problem with Sarah, you simply tell her, right?"

"Yes, and usually we talk about it a while and then resolve it." The light was coming on. "We can do it because we are both in a healthy, adult 'place,' right? Sometimes I do that 'Silent Rebellious Teenager,' but she won't let me get away with it. She just 'hangs out' with me until I'm ready and able to talk with her about the issue. I think I'm getting this."

"It will get clearer and clearer for you as you use the model, Samantha. This healthy, adult 'place' is a state of mind in which we are being proactive and not reactive. When two adults have a problem, they simply talk it out. It may not be easy, as both people usually have pretty strong feelings. That is normal. But you keep talking until both people feel that the issues bothering them are resolved."

"I know I can explain this to Sarah and it will make our relationship even better. I'm not so sure about my parents though." I was really skeptical.

"Samantha, you begin practicing with Sarah. It sounds like your parents have a harder time finding that adult state of mind. We'll work on skills next time for dealing with them. For now, just remember, what they say and do has *nothing to do with you*—you are simply the trigger for their regression. They have their old issues that they are trying to resolve inside themselves. You just keep working on your issues so that you can get control of your life."

"Okay, time's up for today. I'm sorry I talked so much, but I needed to give you the building blocks to help you sort through some of the events of your life. Most of what I've said is on the handouts that I've given you. Keep journaling, especially when you are feeling angry. There's a format for how to journal in the packet. (Maggie's format for journaling is in Appendix III.) And, keep working on the breathing. The breathing is a key ingredient to staying grounded and in the moment. Think of the breathing as putting a patch over the hole in your boundary. Or think of it as putting on the brakes when one of those 'reactive' sub-personalities seems to be heading for a cliff."

Maggie stood up, signaling that our session was over. "I'll see you next week."

"Thanks so much, Maggie. I'm so excited about all this. I really like having the homework. It feels like I'm learning so much. Then I actually get to do something with it, like journaling, which helps me learn it even quicker. I would never have believed that I could feel this way about therapy. Thanks so much! I'll see you next week." I smiled all the way back to work.

chapter 5

"HI, KAY, WHAT'S up?" Since my sister never calls me, I knew as soon as I saw her name on caller ID that she was up to something. I was on my way to work and she must have just dropped the kids off.

"Oh, I just wondered how you are doing. You were really upset the other night, and I haven't talked to you since. Are you okay?"

I felt my gut turn over. *Wow! I'm beginning to recognize a 'set up.'* My sister is really sneaky. The real issue is that I haven't called or stopped by the folks, but she would never just say that. Of course, she and Mom have talked, and Mom has put her up to calling me to 'feel me out.' *What a pair—like two peas in a pod.*

"Of course, I'm okay. I've been super busy at work. What's up with you?" I decided not to play this time. If Kay was going to try to get something out of me, she was going to have to work for it.

Without a pause Kay said, "Well, I've been talking to Mom and she is really upset that you haven't come by or called."

Here we go—the guilt trip. No conversation with Kay or Mom is complete without the guilt trip. Mom and Kay work like a tag team on me. In the past, it has worked—I've always been a sucker and given in to them. Today, I don't think I'm going there.

"Is something happening that I should know about?" I kept my voice very neutral—probably just to irritate Kay. *This is sort of fun!*

"Well, what's happening, Samantha, is that you need to get over it, stop pouting, and act like an adult. Geez, you are behaving like one of my kids. Mom and Dad have the right to give Brian anything they want to."

Kay never called me 'Samantha' unless she was really angry—just like Mom. *Wow! These two really are joined at the hip.* I made a quick decision to bring the temperature of the conversation down.

"Kay, can I be honest with you?" I probably should have known better, but that's what sisters are for aren't they—to confide in? Maybe I just wanted to try one last time to connect with her. I think I really wanted to know if we had any kind of a real relationship or if we just played at it because we were "family."

"Of course you can, Sammy. You should know that by now." I could tell by the tone of her voice that I had her complete attention. Kay continued in a voice that was dripping with sweetness, dying to know what was going on. "Haven't I always been here for you?"

I just spit it out. "I'm in therapy." I waited for the reaction. When I got nothing, I started to wonder if I'd lost her. "Kay, are you there? Did I lose you? Damn cell phones!" I almost drove off the road checking to see if I'd lost my connection.

"No, I'm here. I'm just shocked. Did you say you're in therapy? What in the world for? My God, Samantha, you had the perfect childhood! Dad and Mom were the best parents you could have asked for. Why in the world would you go into therapy?"

In what seemed like a heartbeat, Kay screeched, "You're gay! Oh, my God, you're gay and you're trying to figure out how to tell Mom and Dad. I should have known. You and Sarah have always been just a little too close for my money. I told Mom when you guys were in high school and did everything together that something was going on. You two were always just a little too close. I knew it! You brought home lots of guys but never really pursued a real relationship. That was just to throw us off the track. I was right all along!"

Kay seemed to be off on a planet of her own making. I wasn't sure I could rein her in. "Kay! Whoa! I'm not gay! Jesus, God in Heaven! What started that rant? Is that what you think—that I'm gay? You really don't have any idea who I am, do you? Even if I was gay, would that be such a big deal? I'm not, but why would you go there? Is that what you and Mom talk about? Well, you can relax and tell her I like men and that Sarah and I are really just friends. You two make quite a pair." I was so angry at the thought of Kay and Mom talking about me behind my back that I wanted to spit—especially about something as personal as my sexuality.

"Well, why else would you go to therapy?" Kay said, spitting the words like gun fire.

"Kay, going to therapy does not have to be a bad thing. I've learned so much already. For example, have you ever thought that Dad might be an alcoholic?" I stopped breathing as soon as I had said it. *Why did I open that can of worms? I really am nuts!*

"That is ridiculous! What kind of nonsense is this person filling your head with? I can't believe that you would ever betray our family like this. You better quit this therapy thing right now. There is absolutely nothing wrong with our family! And, I won't let you talk about Daddy like that. After all he's done for all of us. He's worked his butt off his whole life for us, and this is the thanks he gets from you. This is unbelievable! Well, I'm glad that you *aren't* talking to Mom. It would kill her if she knew that you were seeing a therapist who is manipulating you like this. I just can't believe you'd do this to the family. You *are* sick. And, this person sure isn't going to help you!"

I could hear the anger in Kay's voice. She was seething. She was saying exactly what mom would have said if I had told her. Maybe Kay heard Mom's voice in her head, like I did, and it had blended with her own so there was no difference now. At least I couldn't tell anymore where one started and the other left off. *This clearly isn't going anywhere.*

"Okay then, maybe we should change the subject. How are the kids?" I was hoping we could just move on and forget I ever mentioned this therapy thing.

"The kids are fine—like you really care." Kay continued. "You have never been a real aunt to them. You do all the perfunctory things like go to ball games and their school events, but you don't really care. If you did, you would spend more time with them."

"I'm at work now, Kay." *Thank God!* I thought. "I've got to run. Maybe we can talk about this later." As I said it, I thought to myself—*over my dead body!*

I practically kicked myself in the butt as I walked up the stair to my office. If it was physically possible, I would have tried. *What was I thinking?* This was not a subject I could talk to my sister about. *I should know that I can only talk to Sarah about stuff like this.* As I said the words, I realized that the connection I felt to Sarah was what I imagined a 'real' sister relationship to be. *Wow! What an eye-opener. I'll have to tell Sarah when I get home—if she's home and not out with Tim again. Geez, we still haven't talked about the 'Tim thing.' Wonder where this is going?*

As I reached my desk, the phone was ringing. Joann greeted me with, "Sam, can you come to my office right now?" She sounded a little stressed so I skipped my coffee—asking myself as I went, "Can I think without coffee?"—and headed straight for her office. I passed Janet in the hall who just shrugged her shoulders. I mimed drinking a cup of coffee and begging as I passed her, so hopefully she'd take pity on me and bring me some. What would I do without her?

"What's up, Boss?" I asked as I entered Joann's office.

"Have you been working on the Simpson file?"

"Yes. It's almost done, but I still need a couple of days. I have several other things I'm working on, too." I was puzzled about what the rush was. "We weren't supposed to have the work to the Simpson Group until Friday."

"They need it now. They had some sort of change in their production schedule." Joann was clearly frustrated.

I could feel the panic start to rise in my chest. *Wait. Breathe deeply,* I told myself. I took a couple of seconds to get a breath. As luck would have it, Janet walked in with my coffee right then and one for Joann as well. It was a break for me. *Breathe and think.*

After a sip of coffee and a couple of deep breaths, I was able to respond. "Joann, I could probably get the Simpson file done today if I had someone like Janet to help me. I can't possibly do that and the other stuff on my desk without some help. What do you think?"

"Janet, can you reallocate your workload to help Sammy today?"

"It will take some juggling. I'll call accounting to see if they can wait on a couple of things they were pressing me for. I don't think it will be a problem, but it would help if you called Sue and gave her a 'heads up'."

"Sure, I'll call right now. Both of you need to tell me what I can do to help. I'll clear out my late afternoon schedule, so call if you need me for *anything*."

Janet was out the door.

"Thanks, Samantha. I always know I can count on you to help me figure something out." Joann was obviously relieved.

I walked out the door and worked like a dog until 7:00 that night beside Janet and Joann, but the job was done and ready to present to the client the next morning. I headed for home, letting Lizzie have her head, as they used to say about horses. I swear to God this car really does know its way home when I'm exhausted or on emotional overload.

Oh shit! I am supposed to journal. I was a really good client for Maggie DeWitt because even I knew I was somewhat obsessive-compulsive. There was no way that I was going to show up for that therapy appointment without having done my homework. *Well, at least I had lots of good stuff to journal about, given that exchange with Kay this morning. Wow, that seemed like a long time ago. Can that just have been twelve hours ago? I hope I can remember it all. Sarah is going to be rolling on the floor with this one.*

"What a sweetheart you are!" I said to Sarah as I walked in the door. I could smell dinner before I hit the doorway. There are some times when I feel overwhelmed by her kindness to me—this was one of them. "I have had a bitch of a day. Thank you so much for thinking about food. I'd probably have eaten a peanut butter sandwich and called it a day—well no, I still have to journal. You aren't going to believe what Kay said to me this morning while I was driving to work."

Sarah just looked at me with that sweet face of hers after I had recounted my 'little talk' with Kay. "You amaze me, Sam. I could have told you that your family has thought that about us for years. Why do you think I stay away from them? I think they see me as the one who 'led you astray.' Your family is really strange—nice, but strange. I have just tried to listen to you and hoped that you'd start to see it one day."

"Sarah, I don't know what to say. I don't know whether to be mad at you for not saying anything or thankful that I've had you as a best friend all these years. Mostly, I just appreciate you for hanging out with me through all the garbage they dish out. It can't have been easy for you. Hey, you know what I discovered today? I figured out that you are my 'real' sister, not Kay. Okay, you're way ahead of me again. I can see it by that dopey look on your face. You probably have thought that for a long time. Right? Are you sitting there wondering how I could be so dumb?"

"Oh, Sam, you know me better than that. I've just always believed that when you were ready it would hit you—sort of like it is right now. For some reason you are ready now to deal with your parents and the rest of your family. It has really hurt to see some of the things that they have done to you, but I couldn't fix it—only you could, when you finally started to see it. Seems to me like the time has come. I'm so happy for you, Sammy."

"Thanks, Sarah. You know what? I'm happy for me too! Hey, it's getting late, and I have to write. No way am I going to that appointment without doing my homework. We need to talk about Tim one of these days. Is this thing getting serious?"

"Yes, but we aren't talking about it now. You need to journal, or you'll be mad at yourself for a week. Maybe we can talk tomorrow night when you aren't home so late. Write! Write! I'll bring you some tuna casserole when it's done." Sarah was out of the room in a flash leaving me with nothing but my journal and Shiloh.

Being new to this journaling thing, I didn't know where to begin. I took out the sheet Maggie had given me. What was I feeling this morning during the talk with Kay? I was feeling manipulated—no, she said think basic feelings like happy, sad, angry, or scared. Well, I wasn't happy that's for sure. I didn't cry so I guess I wasn't sad. I think I was angry. Well, I know I was angry because she was so judgmental and so in my face about knowing me when she doesn't know shit about me. I was also angry when she made it all about 'the family' and what I was doing to them. "What about me? Don't I count for anything?" I felt angry just saying that. Basically, I don't have a right to take care of myself. Somehow it's my job to take care of her and the whole rest of the family.

The more I wrote, the madder I got. Sarah started in the door with a plate and I waved her away. I was on a roll. I ended up writing a letter to Kay. I found it kind of interesting. In the past I just 'stuffed' it when I got angry or took it out on Sarah by yelling and screaming around the house. I don't think I'd ever just focused the anger on the person I was angry at. This felt really good. It helped to think back to all the times that she had pulled dirty tricks on me or done something wrong and then blamed it on me. Mom always bought Kay's and Brian's stories. I was the one that was the "instigator," as she used to call me.

I remembered one night when we were doing dishes after supper. Kay dropped one of Mom's favorite bowls. Mom came running into the kitchen and Kay yelled, "Sam pushed me, Mom." I got the smack in the face and sent to my room. I still remember the smell of popcorn as they all sat in the living room eating popcorn and watching television. "What a bitch you are, Kay!" I said to the room in general.

"I like the sound of this," Sarah yelled from the living room. I hadn't realized that my door was open.

"I was just remembering a time when I got the blame for something Kay did. Remembering all this stuff makes me angry and hungry."

"Want some tuna now or popcorn?" It was time to calm down so that I could get some sleep. I headed for the kitchen. Sarah followed me.

"Tuna feels too heavy and you know I'm always up for popcorn." I actually felt lighter as I walked into the kitchen.

"What was the big deal that went down at work today?" Sarah asked as she got the popcorn out.

She was always eager to hear about my job. She worked with all men, in stark contrast to my all-female working environment. She really enjoyed listening to my stories and visa versa. Our worlds were so completely different.

"You know it is not so much what the problem was, but how we handled it." I was excited as I thought about what healthy adult women we all were today in that office. "God, it could have been really ugly, Sarah. I felt myself start to panic when Joann was getting stressed out and needed something ASAP. I literally felt my teeth clench, and I could have easily just lost it—especially on top of the shit my sister had just thrown at me. But I didn't lose it. I actually reminded myself to breathe. It was kind of cool because Janet brought coffee at a pivotal moment so that both Joann and I took a little time out from the stress."

"Then the three of us just stood there and processed what each of us could do and when, so that we could get this one client taken care of without any of us really having to bear the brunt of the problem. I could really see the model that Dr. DeWitt talked about in my head. We all stayed adult. All of us talked about our needs, but we also listened to each other's needs. Then we sort of all negotiated without calling it that, of course, and figured out what to do."

"It was really pretty amazing. I always knew I loved my job, but today is a perfect example of *why* I love my job so much. I feel so good working with these women. Oh, we have our bad days and times but mostly we are just a team—and a mighty good team, I might add."

"Sounds like I need to hear more about this therapy with Dr. DeWitt. I might help me with all the men in my office. We've got to schedule some time for *us* in the next week or so. We've just both been so busy. You need popcorn and bed right now though," Sarah concluded.

"This popcorn is yummy. You put way too much butter on it—just the way I love it. Thanks so much, Sarah, for everything."

"Are you kidding, Sam—I love the butter as much as the popcorn, too. And I love you! So you think this thing with Tim is getting serious, do you? Well, I think it might be. He is so sweet to me. He's the first one that I've ever really been able to see myself with in the future. It just feels right, Sammy. I'm sort of scared though. Besides my grandmother, you are my closest family. How does a guy fit into our lives?"

I could see that Sarah was serious and somewhat concerned. I wasn't exactly sure what she was concerned about, but I knew that what she was contemplating meant change and neither of us handled change well. "You know what? We can figure this out and if Tim's the guy you think he is, he'll be here figuring it out with us. I'm heading for bed, girlfriend. I'm exhausted. We'll talk more tomorrow."

Shiloh did her usual turning around in circles routine that she did when Sarah and I went to bed at the same time. It drove her crazy because she couldn't decide which of us to sleep with. "Oh come with me you crazy mutt. Sarah's bed is going to be too full for you in the near future. We both better start getting used to it."

chapter 6

"You are amazing, Samantha." Doctor DeWitt was literally beaming at me. "It is so easy to work with you. You are so motivated. It's great that you saw through Kay's manipulations early so that you could be more boundaried with her. I'm also glad to hear that the journaling helped you to deal with your anger at your sister. I like how you came to the awareness that dealing with her directly, by writing, is more beneficial to you than yelling at the dog or stomping around the apartment. Since dealing with anger is one of the things you want to work on, we'll just focus on anger this session."

"Before we get into *how* to deal with your anger, maybe we should look at *why* you might be so angry. Have you ever really thought much about your childhood before? Obviously, this event with your sister triggered lots of old memories. Tell me about the anger in your home and how you dealt with it?"

"The crazy thing is that I don't really remember feeling angry. I thought I was the happiest person I knew. I guess I did what you said in the first session. I just stuffed it, sort of felt nothing, and then I exploded. Unfortunately, as you know, I usually exploded at all the wrong people. I don't think I have ever in my life said that I was angry out loud. I can remember my mother screaming at us kids, but we were never allowed to talk back and we were never allowed to be angry. The only person in our home who could get angry was Mom. She only yelled at us kids, though. When she was mad at Dad, it was the silent treatment."

"Maggie, I can see the model in my head now. I can see myself under the glass and all the parts. I can also see it in other people. My mom was the Rebellious Teenager with us kids, but she was the Silent Rebellious Teenager with Dad. And my dad, wow, he just never said anything. I have no idea whether he was angry or not. He was just totally 'shut down' and he withdrew. I guess that is also the Silent Rebellious Teenager. Well, now I see why I don't know how to say a simple, 'I'm angry.' I have never heard anyone talk like that."

"It's funny, when Sarah and I have a conflict; I want to retreat into my bedroom, like I said last time. I want to run away and hope that it will just go away—do that flight thing. She won't let that happen. She follows me. We usually just talk and talk until we are not angry any more. I can't remember really staying angry at her for any long period of time. It would sure be a lot easier if I could learn to confront problems with people instead of just hoping they will go away by themselves, because they never do. I've learned that much already."

"Samantha, give yourself a break. You are just learning this stuff. Here's a little formula you can use in the future. I'll write it on the board, and I'll give you a handout so that when you guys have a disagreement you can use it." (This formula is found in Appendix IV.)

When you say or do….(Be specific.)

I feel…(Happy, sad, angry, or scared)

Because I imagine…(Tell her what you are telling yourself about what is happening.)

What I need from you now is…(Be specific.)

What I need in the future is…(Be specific.)

"Let me give you an example to make that clearer. Let's say that the two of you had planned to meet after work for a drink, and Sarah forgot. The way that you handle it is to say to her: 'Sarah, when you forget an event we've planned, I feel angry. I feel angry because I tell myself that you don't care about me, that I'm not important to you.' Then you would listen to her response. If she offers a good reason for forgetting, you may not need much of anything after that. What you might need in that moment is an apology and then reassurance that something like that won't happen again. A lot of it depends on what is happening as you dialogue."

"Does this sound like something you could try with Sarah?" Maggie asked.

"I think I could do it with her," I responded. "It might sound silly to you, but I think I'll be very scared to try something like this. I'm just not a direct person. I usually avoid conflict if I can. It seems like it would be easier in the long run, but way harder in the beginning. Sarah is really a safe person for me, so maybe I should tell her about it ahead of time and sort of prepare her for it. Then I could just tell her, 'Hey, I need to try that new formula.' I think she would be more than willing. I actually think she likes the stuff you are doing with me. I tell her everything, and she seems to be learning, too. It's fun to do this with someone you live with."

Maggie laughed. "Well, some of the couples I counsel might not agree with you. I think it's fun when you don't trigger each other—otherwise it is nothing but really hard work. There is an example in the handout I gave you to make it a little easier. Actually, the example you gave me of the dialogue you had with your boss and co-worker was very healthy. Maybe if a situation comes up at work, you could try it there, too. I encourage people to leave out the 'because I imagine' line at work because that is usually information that co-workers don't need. Save that for the significant people in your life with whom you want to create intimacy. Any questions about that, or are you ready to move on?" Maggie asked.

"Are you saying that I shouldn't try this with my family?" I wasn't clear whether this was something I should be doing with *most* people or just a few select people.

"Remember what you said about feeling scared when you thought about trying this with Sarah? Well, that is normal because this is not how you are accustomed to talking to people—think of it as learning a new language. You wouldn't try to speak a new language in front of people who you thought might ridicule you, would you? Of course not, so just try this with people that you already feel comfortable with—people who are already pretty healthy and who will appreciate doing things differently if it will improve communication. I'm not saying, 'Don't do it,' with your family. I'm saying, 'Try it first with the easiest people.' Does that make it clearer, Samantha?"

"Yes, and I know you are right." I found myself tearing up for some unknown reason. "I just wish I could get it right with my mom and dad. I want so much just to be loved the way they love Kay and Brian. I don't get what is so wrong with me that I'm treated differently."

"It's okay to cry, Samantha. It is sad that your relationship isn't what you want it to be with your parents and your siblings."

For some reason, hearing that it was okay to cry just felt like it went right to my core. I guess I had heard for so long, "Stop crying or I'll give you something to cry about," that this seemed like permission to feel—to just be myself. All the flood gates broke, and I just cried and cried. Maggie didn't say a word, and yet I have never felt so taken care of and supported.

It seemed like I cried forever, but I'm sure it was probably only a few minutes. "I'm sorry. I just don't know what came over me." I don't know why I felt a need to apologize. Maggie was sympathetic and empathetic.

"You don't need to apologize for being real, Samantha. You felt sad and you cried. You can't get any more authentic than that. Somewhere along the line you got the message that you shouldn't cry. Whoever gave you that message was wrong. Remember in our first session I said the way to know yourself is to know what you feel. Well, if people are telling you not to feel, they stop your growth process. And when they do it over and over, it makes it almost impossible to learn what feelings are and how to deal with them."

"Now you have to go back and work through all those feelings that you stuffed. You stuffed them somewhere. Remember, you said that you have a whole filing cabinet full of events that you have never allowed yourself to have feelings about. You'll have more times like you just experienced. I just hope that today has been a good model of how to deal with those events. Just let yourself feel your feelings and get support."

Maggie continued, "Getting support is difficult sometimes. Do you think that Sarah would be able to sit with you like I just did, not forever but at least a time or two while you are learning to do this?"

"Well, I don't know for sure, but if I explain it to her, I think she would. Why is having support so important? Why can't I just do this myself? I have never been very good at asking people for support or help or anything for that matter. I'm sort of an 'I can do it myself' kind of person." I wasn't liking this idea of asking anybody for anything, even Sarah.

"Why does that answer not surprise me in the least?" Maggie laughed out loud. "This is a little complicated, but it is really important. If I lose you, yell."

"When you were a child, what you needed was for your mother and the other important adults in your life to just hear you and validate your feelings—even if they didn't agree with them. For example, if you wanted to eat a whole bag of cookies your mom had put in the grocery cart while shopping and your mom said, 'No,' you had a right to be angry at her for not giving them to you. I'm not saying she should have given them to you. I'm saying you had a right to be angry because you couldn't have them. A healthy mom would have simply stayed with you while you threw your tantrum. She might have rubbed your back or just said, 'I hear how mad you are at Mama. You have a right to be mad.' Or perhaps she would have just taken you from the store and talked to you in the car. That is called 'presence.' Good parenting is about presence."

"There are many things that parents have to teach their children. Some of the most important lessons have to do with teaching children about their feelings. That is good parenting. First, parents have to teach the child the label for the feelings she's having. That's why I said that the parent should say something like 'I hear you are mad at Mama.' The parent is teaching the child that the feeling she is experiencing is anger."

"Second," Maggie continued, "the parent needs to validate that those feelings are appropriate—even if, and maybe especially if, the parent is not going to give in to the child's wish. When the parent can do this, it's not about a power struggle. It's about a teaching moment. I have children, so I know how hard it is to take advantage of those teaching moments. Often, it is just easier to take the cookies, put them on the shelf, and walk out of the store. It is hard to stay present to a small child, honoring them and their wishes. At the same time, that is exactly what the child needs."

"If the parent or adult figure doesn't teach her, then the child tries to understand what is going on by herself. It is impossible for a child to understand because it only has one worldview, it's own—children are egocentric. You were a child, Samantha. You couldn't have known the problems with your request for a whole bag of cookies. You needed an adult voice to put a label on what was happening—you were angry. You also needed an adult to say, 'It's okay to be angry.' When you didn't get that, you started taking care of yourself. Perhaps, the Internal Critic said, 'You don't deserve cookies. Or the young Rebellious Teenager said, 'I didn't want those stupid cookies anyway.' Whatever you did to make yourself feel better, it was the best you could do as a child."

"You were smart enough to know that if you didn't take care of yourself, nobody else would. The problem is that the inner voice is only a child, too. The logic is always faulty because it is created in a child's mind. Just because a child is smart, it doesn't mean that she or he has the capacity to be an adult. It is still a child's mind; concrete, black-and-white thinking is all she's able to do. The child figures out that she's on her own—hence the 'I can do it myself; I don't need anybody.' And the child spends the rest of her life '*acting as if*' she is an adult, rather than actually growing into one."

"Maggie, are you saying that my problems are all my parents' fault?" I think I was starting to feel a little defensive for my parents.

"No, Samantha, that is not what I'm saying. I'm sure that your parents did the very best that they could do. That doesn't mean that they did a great job. Not because they are bad people, but because they are human. They were raised by people who were human who had issues—and the family has just passed those issues down, generation to generation, finally to you. I don't want you to think about your issues in terms of blame. I want you to think about it as holding your parents accountable. In the places they did a poor job, you need to be able to say—perhaps not to them directly but at least to yourself—I'm angry that you didn't know how to parent me better in this particular situation. Overall, your parents did a good job. Look at you: you are bright, witty, and successful in many ways. At the same time, they have hurt you. You have a right to be angry about the times they have hurt you."

"As and example," Maggie added, "If your dad had worked three jobs to make enough money so the family could eat, but was never home, you have a right to be angry. As an adult you know that it was rational for him to be gone—you needed food more than you needed to play with your dad. But as a child you didn't have that kind of ability to be rational. All you knew is that you had no dad and other kids did. You have a right to voice that anger. In some ways, I think people have a responsibility to express their anger because otherwise it 'leaks out' in other ways—passive-aggressive ways. Perhaps you'd leak anger at Dad by forgetting his birthday or something like that."

I was feeling a little clearer but still needed more information, "Maggie, do you think that my mom was really angry at my dad but just didn't know how to tell him, so she 'leaked' on to us kids?"

"Well, that is really hard to say," Maggie responded. "There are so many other factors at work. There is just no way to guess what was happening with her. That is why your job is to focus on you. It is really important that you understand the notion of 'righteous anger' though because I want your journaling to focus on your anger. I want you to go back and look at some of those entries from before and do something similar to the writing you did about Kay. Write the anger you have about your mom or dad or whoever deserves your anger. Just keep going through those file drawers. You may remember events from school with teachers; the possibilities are endless. Use any memory that 'pops up.' I just want you to pick events and then write your anger directly to the person. Start with, 'When I think about…., I feel angry.' Then just write until you've said everything that the parts of you needed to say back then. Use the format for journaling so that you let all the voices speak."

"That Rebellious Teenager is an important part of your personality," Maggie continued. "She has been protecting you for a long time. She has a right to a voice. You have sort of kept her in the closet for all these years. She gets fed up, and out she pops with years of anger exploding out of her. She doesn't know how else to express herself. You are now giving her the opportunity to speak without censure—but ONLY to you. I can't stress enough that she can only talk to *you*. That's why I said you have a right to say this stuff—any way you want to, 'Fuck You's' included. You just don't have a right to expose other people to that kind of behavior—not even your dog." We both laughed at that.

"Think of it this way. When that Teenager yells and screams, she gives the 'adult' you the information she needs to handle situations appropriately. If you don't know you are angry, you'll let someone walk on you and then 'leak' with someone else. If you let yourself feel the anger and express it, in the privacy of your own home, then you can confront the individual with whom you have a problem and speak to that person from a healthy, grounded, adult place. Now we are back to that formula that I gave you to try with Sarah. You can use that with anyone if you are in a fully informed place. In that healthy place you know yourself and can trust that you will 'represent yourself' as the powerful adult woman that you are."

"Let me give you an example from my own life. My husband snapped at me the other morning. Remember, I told you I have issues with loud, male voices. I regressed immediately and then wouldn't talk to him—that would be the Silent Rebellious Teenager acting out. After some time, I saw clearly that I had been triggered. I did a little feeling work, trying to process what was happening. I felt really sad and asked him to hold me. I cried about how much my dad had hurt me—that was the Regressed 'little' part. He held me and was very supportive."

"I thought I was finished with the issue, and so we went walking. On the walk, I heard the Rebellious Teenager say, 'I'm so pissed! I don't need this shit! I don't need him. He's a jerk.' Hearing her words, I knew that I was not finished with the issue after all. I knew that I had to confront my husband about his behavior."

"I was able to do it as an adult though," Maggie continued. "I simply used the formula I gave you. I said to him, 'When you snap at me using that tone of voice, I feel really, really angry. I need to hear that you are sorry you snapped at me this morning and I need to know that you will try not to use that tone with me in the future.' Of course he apologized immediately and also reassured me that he would work on his tone of voice. Do you think you are clear enough about this to try it out this week?" Maggie asked.

"Yes, that example helped. That's how I want to be able to interact with people. Are you sure I can sort out these voices in my head? I feel like I'm running Samantha's kindergarten. I know I hear the different voices, but I'm not so sure I can sort them out when each one is demanding to get her need met first."

"This will get easier the longer you do it. I promise," Maggie continued. "Listen for key sentences. The Regressed part is the one who feels four years old and says, 'I don't know what to do.' The Silent Rebellious Teenager is the one who wants to run away while doing lots of angry, blaming, 'you statements' in her head. The Rebellious Teenager is the one who says, 'I don't need anyone. I can take care of myself.' She does this out loud and directly to the person if they are within earshot. And, remember she is the one who does all the swearing. The Internal Critic is the one who is saying all those 'you should' messages to you and about you. I promise that as you begin to hear them as distinct voices, it will get easier."

"Oh, I don't want to forget to answer your question about support—in the long run the adult Samantha will be all the support you need—in the short run, you need someone to model what support looks like, in part, because you didn't get it as a child. Support is another word for 'presence.' Sarah will work perfectly because she's safe and she's a good friend. All she has to do is listen, like I did, and stay present. Tell her that means she doesn't get to daydream. You may not need her at all; but if you start to feel sad, please don't just cry by yourself—you're already an expert at that. Ask her to just spend some time with you while you cry."

"Is there anything else that you need to know before we end the session?" Maggie asked.

"Only, where does the time go? It seems like I just got here. Wow, this was really interesting. I'll do the journaling every night—oh, I know, I don't need to tell you that. You already can see how compulsive I am about it. It just really helps me. Sarah wanted me to tell you that I have my clothes on color-coordinated hangers. She thinks that says something about me." I laughed as I said it.

"It only confirms that you are a perfectionist, my dear, and probably a bit of a control freak. I'm so glad we're working on emotional control. That had to really bother you. I have a hunch it's not okay for Samantha to be less than perfect." Maggie got up and walked to the door.

"See you next week, or do you want to make it two weeks—more time to practice?" Maggie opened the door for me.

"No. I'll be here next week, same time. Thanks so much." I was out the door feeling like I was on an adventure. I kind of felt like my life was like that show, "The New Adventures of Somebody or Other," except it was me. I liked the sound of that, "The New Adventures of Samantha Daley."

chapter 7

MY HEAD WAS a jumble of thoughts as I drove home. Work had been a no-brainer, so I basically spent the afternoon rehashing everything Maggie had said. *What am I feeling? Why is it so hard to figure out what I feel?* Some part of me was like the little kid in the first row, *"I know, I know!"*

Okay, I know she said that I wasn't ever really taught what feelings were and what to do with them. When they came up, I stuffed them because the feelings confused me and made me uncomfortable. Those same feelings seemed to make all the adults in my life angry. So maybe that's why feelings still make me feel uncomfortable. I sure don't handle it well when other people get sad or mad. So, I think I get all that. How do I start figuring out what I feel? In other words—how do I start figuring out who I am? This could be harder than it seemed when Maggie and I first explored this topic.

I saw Tim's car when I pulled into my parking spot. *I wonder if they are going out or staying in tonight.* I wasn't sure I was up to watching a movie as a threesome. The stuff from my session was still swirling around in my brain, and I sort of wanted to do some journaling. I wanted to get started on "cleaning out the filing cabinets"—I liked the image of that, neat freak that I am.

"Hi guys," I yelled as I walked in. Shiloh came running. She was always looking for food and when someone walked in the door, she was always pretty sure that food was walking in the door, too. Given our lifestyles, she was usually right. "I didn't bring anything home. Sorry, Baby." I rubbed her ears hoping to make up for my *faux pas*. Shiloh was having none of it. She turned her back on me and ran to burrow her head in the couch—got to be some popcorn left from the last movie. She was a dog on a mission.

Tim and Sarah were sitting at the kitchen table. They looked like they had been deep in some conversation. "Am I interrupting something?" I asked as I headed for my bedroom. "I have homework from my shrink." I was hoping that this would be seen as letting them have their space as well as me getting some space for myself.

Sarah hopped up from the chair. "Sammy, come sit for a minute." Something in the way she said it caused my stomach to do a flip-flop.

"What's up?" I asked. "Is something's wrong?" I had a bad feeling about whatever it was that was going on. I moved toward the couch and sat down, ignoring Shiloh, who just continued to dig.

"Nothing's 'wrong', Sam. It's just that Tim and I have been talking. We've dated on and off for a year and in the last few months things have gotten much more serious. We are talking about living together to see how that goes, like as a next step. Neither one of us feels ready for marriage, but we do feel like we might be headed in that direction." They had moved to the loveseat across from me.

"You and Granny are the two most important people in my life. I haven't lived with anyone but you since we graduated from high school. I just don't want to make this decision without including you. Tim and I both want to know how you feel about it. And frankly, we are kind of looking for ideas or suggestions. We don't know whether we should both move into Tim's place or if he should move in here with us. We just aren't sure what would feel right for you…Help me here, Sam. Say something." Sarah pleaded.

I felt like I had just been run over by something very big. It didn't help that during Sarah's outburst, Shiloh had decided to sit right on me. They say dogs know when something's going on. Shiloh sure seemed to, and I could tell she was on my side. I don't think she liked how close Tim was sitting to Sarah—that was her spot.

"Well, give me time to get a breath," I said while shoving Shiloh off me. "And I need a little space so I can breathe, please, girl. Okay, let me get this straight. You guys have decided to move in together. As I hear it, the issue is where to live. And somehow I'm supposed to know what I think about this right now? Well, I just don't know what to say. I don't know how I feel about it. It seems to me if you want to do it, do it! It's none of my business. I certainly don't need you to stay here. I can handle this place by myself." *Hmmm. Weren't those some of the words I was supposed to listen for… fuck that, I don't care.*

"How do I *feel* about it? Well, frankly right now the idea feels like crap and I don't want to talk about it." I jumped up and headed for my room.

"Sammy, please!" I heard Sarah, but I just wasn't in the mood, not in front of Tim anyway. I shut the door behind me hoping that there would be a small earthquake and that side of the apartment would sort of fall off, and then I'd be by myself. A few minutes later I heard the apartment door close and Sarah knocking on my door.

"Tim's gone. Can we talk now?" Sarah asked tearfully. When I opened the door, Sarah was standing there with big tears running down her face. "I'm so sorry, Sammy. I shouldn't have sprung it on you with Tim here. It's just that you mentioned the three of us being able to talk about stuff, and I got this idea that it might be good to have him here while we talked about it. See, he and I have been talking about it for a while. I just kind of forgot that you haven't been in the loop. This had to come as quite a shock. I'm sorry. Can we talk about it now? I promise I'll slow down so you can catch up."

"I don't know, Sarah. Just give me a few minutes to change out of my work clothes and get comfortable. This has been quite the homecoming. Just let me get used to the idea for a minute." I was snapping at her, but I could feel my energy level dropping. I started out feeling really, really angry. Now, something was shifting. *Wow, this must have hit a really big hole in my boundary.*

"I'll go get us a Coke and a snack. You get comfortable. I'll be back in a couple minutes," Sarah said as she left my room. *How does she always know that a little caffeine and food will work wonders on my sense of well-being?* It did feel good to just put on sweats and get my make up off. *Ahhh… that's better. Why does everything seem better once you get your pantyhose off? Maybe I feel better because I really can take a deep breath.*

"Hey, are you decent?" Sarah called as she opened the door. "I've got a little snack ready. It's on the table in the kitchen. If we don't hurry, Shiloh will beat us to it." Since we both know our pooch, we headed for the kitchen at high speed. As we sat eating, I could feel myself calming down. I was breathing again and not feeling nearly as triggered and "little" as I had earlier.

"You know the first thing that came up for me, Sarah, when you were asking how I felt about it, was Dr. DeWitt saying, 'Start with the words, when I think about…, I feel.' At first I was just shocked and angry that you had sprung it on me. But, now when I think about you leaving, what I really feel is scared. We've been together for so long; I'm scared to try living my life without you. I'm not stupid. I knew that some day one of us would find someone and have to leave. I guess I always thought I'd do it first. Don't ask me why I thought that with all the loser guys I've dragged through here. You seem to find all the nice ones and then dump them."

"Sammy, I'm scared, too. I'm scared to let Tim too far into my life because I'm afraid I'll get hurt like I was hurt when my parents were killed. I think that's why I've been running from relationships. You getting into therapy has kind of triggered a lot of old memories of stuff I did in therapy after they died. It has pushed me to see that I can't continue to live my life in fear of people leaving me. In some ways our relationship has made me believe that not everyone who loves me leaves or ends up hurting me."

"I think, too," Sarah continued, "that in some ways I've believed I was taking care of you, Sammy. I made my staying about you needing me because you really didn't have anyone else. As I see you change because of the therapy, I see you as more able to take care of yourself. I guess you always have been able to take care of yourself. We just seem to have a lot of fun taking care of each other. So what do you think?"

"First of all, I want to say I think Tim is absolutely wonderful. He is one of the nicest guys you've ever dated. So, if you are going to get serious, this is a good one to get serious about. He adores you, and I can see how much you care about him—Sarah, your eyes do that twinkle thing when you talk about him. I need you to give me some time to adjust. I think you two ought to be the ones to decide the living arrangements. We have six months on this lease. I'd have to find someone to sublet your half because I couldn't afford to do it myself—*contrary to what that Teenager said earlier.* It might take me some time to find someone. Are you guys in a rush? Does this have to be a 'right now' decision?"

Sarah had gotten up and was sort of pacing around the room. The excitement was just oozing out of her. "No, we aren't in a rush, *but* Tim's lease is almost up. What do you think about him moving in with us? It would be a way for all of us to get to know each other because you are part of my life, forever, sister dear. If he doesn't like you, well…I just don't know. That just might be the end of the relationship. What do you think? Can we do this, Sammy? This is really what I wanted to try, but I didn't know if you'd be okay—you know, with a man around."

As I watched her pace, I started to feel her excitement. Sarah was so happy that she looked like a child on Christmas morning. Who could throw a wet blanket on all that enthusiasm?—not me. "Oh my God, Sarah, a man in the house! I'll have to wear a bathrobe—do I own a bathrobe? It sounds great to me—sound the trumpets, tell the man he's welcome! I guess we all have about six months to get to know each other and then get used to the idea of you two moving off by yourselves."

"Hey, enough for now! I think this is my cue to go to my room. I have some journaling I want to do. Oh, Sarah, I can't wait till I tell you all the good stuff I learned at this session with Maggie. Of course all that can wait, I believe that you have a telephone call to make—or is he waiting in his car downstairs? Go tell him all's well. He should feel free to start moving in anytime. Don't tell me he's got his stuff in the car though, or I'll think you guys planned this whole thing."

"Don't be silly. We'll probably run to his house for some overnight stuff. We'll be back soon. I love you, my friend." Sarah said, beaming. I got a huge hug and Sarah was out the door like a flash.

I went to the kitchen to make a peanut butter and jelly sandwich. I made one for me and one for Shiloh and we headed back to my bedroom. I had a lot to journal about. Sarah and I had done well, I thought, processing this whole thing. When I started journaling, I got in touch with sadness and anger. It seemed strange to me that the first feeling I got in touch with was fear. Because I'd talked that part through with Sarah, however it had sort of disappeared. I really thought the journaling I did on the anger was interesting, mostly because I discovered I was just angry that she was "leaving me." I sounded a little like Sarah when she was talking about how she felt when her parents died. *This stuff is amazing!*

When the phone rang, I thought it was Sarah so I didn't even look at caller ID—Big Mistake! I didn't expect to hear my mother's voice on the other end of the line. "Oh, you *are* still alive. I thought you were dead. Are you ever going to come over here again?" Mom said, her voice dripping with sarcasm. She was in her martyr mode. I could always tell because of the tone in her voice.

"Hi, Ma, how are you?" It was all I could think to say. *Take a deep breath!*

"Well, I'm not doing very well. I had to visit the doctor because I was having pains in my heart again. He thinks it's stress. He thinks that I got too upset about how you stomped out of the house last weekend. He says that I can't control how you behave and that I should be happy that I have two children who love me and treat me well. He told me not to call you, to let you call me, but I'm a mother. I can't help worrying about you. I had to call." The audible sigh at the other end let me know that she was done trying to make me feel guilty, and now I should begin begging her for forgiveness.

"Mom, I didn't call because I've been busy and because I have some stuff going on in my life. I'm not angry any longer. You and Dad have a right to give Brian and Kay anything you want. I'm okay now, honestly. I'll probably be over sometime this weekend. Are Mike and Kay and the kids coming over Sunday after church?"

"Of course they are." I could hear the smile on her face. "*They* never miss having dinner with us on Sunday—or church either for that matter. Everyone at church asks me where you are. I just pretend I don't hear them because I'm so embarrassed that you don't attend church any more. I'm really worried about you, Samantha."

"Don't worry, Mom. God and I have it covered. I'll try to get over to see you this Sunday. I'll let you know if I'm not going to be able to make it."

I started to journal the minute I hung up the phone. Mom had just opened the file drawer in my head labeled "guilt." I was on a roll. I started writing down all the angry feelings I had about the bazillion times she had laid a guilt trip on me about church attendance, the clothes I wore, how bad I was compared to Brian and Kay. The list went on. So did I. I wrote until my hand was numb, but boy did I feel better! It also felt good to just write the words, "I am so angry at you, Mom." *Wow, what a relief it is to get this stuff out!*

I was just finishing up—actually my hand had betrayed me and was so numb I couldn't write any more—when I heard Sarah and Tim walk in the door.

"Hey, *American Idol* is on. Are you going to come and watch it with us?" Sarah yelled, and Tim followed it up with, "Come out, come out, even without a bathrobe." I heard the two of them burst out laughing. This was going to be a crazy six months.

I was ready to be freed from my 'processing mode.' "I'll get the popcorn going. You might as well get used to it, Tim. We have our rituals around here, and either you get with the program, or you're history." I felt really comfortable kidding Tim. He sort of had "good brother" energy.

"I'll do the butter," Tim said. "Sarah never puts enough butter on the popcorn for me."

Oh, my God, I like this man! I started humming on the way to the kitchen. *Humming—me, humming—now that's interesting.*

I'd have to tell Maggie that all I ever seem to come up with are scared, sad, and angry feelings in my journal, but I'm working on finding the happy feelings and I seem to be getting closer. It seems to get a little easier to write in the journal each time. It is sort of like cleaning out a closet. As I throw out the bad, old stuff, there is more room for the new, happy stuff.

I grabbed my phone as I walked to the living room. They couldn't choose the *American Idol* without my vote.

chapter 8

"Samantha, I just can't believe how much you accomplish in a week. You have no idea how important the work you are doing during the week is in helping you grow." Maggie seemed genuinely pleased with what I had told her about the goings on in my world.

"Can I ask you a question, Maggie?"

"Of course you can. What do you want to know, Samantha?"

"Well, that's it, you always call me Samantha, never Sammy or Sam like everyone else. Is there a reason why? You go by a nickname. I don't care, mind you. It's just different. Usually when people use my full name, they are angry at me."

"Actually, I've chosen to do that on purpose." Maggie actually seemed kind of pleased that I had noticed. "The first time you came in you said that your parents had wanted a boy and then proceeded to tell me I could call you Sam or Sammy. Those are boy's names. I chose to acknowledge you for the woman that you are, Samantha, and that means calling you by a woman's name. And, it's a beautiful name, I might add. It fits you perfectly."

"Oh, my gosh! That is really cool! I love how you explained your reasoning. I certainly had never thought about my nicknames that way. I really would have to say that I've never even thought of myself as a woman. That's kind of for Mom and Grandma. You are so right! I am a woman! At least now I'm actually beginning to feel like one. Samantha Daley, I really like the sound of that. Thanks for explaining your use of my given name. I think I did try to be a boy for my dad—but of course couldn't really pull it off no matter how hard I tried." We both laughed.

"I'd like to revisit our first session, and go over a few things I've been thinking about." Maggie said, speaking in a determined manner. "You brought up topics that would lead me to believe that there are a lot of angry feelings sort of 'floating around' in your family that are never really spoken. For example, you mentioned that both your mother and grandmother were pregnant when they got married. Can you see that people marrying under those circumstances just *might* be angry? The problem is that under those circumstances *a lot* of people are probably angry—the parents of the two getting married, the man and the woman, perhaps others. If no one talks about that anger, it just continues to exist in the void where there are no words. Remember how your scared feelings changed when you talked to Sarah about them. If you hadn't talked to her, you would still have those feelings—only you'd be stuffing them like you used to do—and eventually they would 'leak' out."

"Oh, I totally understand about 'leaking anger' now." I could easily visualize times not only when I had done it but when others had done it to me. "Go on, Maggie." I wanted to hear more.

"I think, perhaps, that those unplanned pregnancies were two of the reasons for the pervasive anger in the house. Then you said you were born a girl, and they were disappointed. When you didn't complete the picture of their perfect family, one girl and one boy, that may have been what caused the anger in the family to be focused on you."

"So, you are saying that the reason for their unhappiness was because I had 'messed it up' for them? When Brian came along the family was perfect—except for this one person in the middle, me." Something seemed to 'click.' I could feel more of the pieces of the puzzle falling into place.

"Yes, you became the one that didn't fit—in their eyes. You somehow became the reason for their discontent. You became the scapegoat. Again, Samantha, I'm just guessing at how the people in your household felt, but given what you've told me and my knowledge of alcoholic families, this probably is pretty close. I also want you to hear loud and clear that I do not believe for a minute that any of this is conscious on the part of anyone in your family. Not one of them thinks, 'Samantha is the misfit in this family.' In fact, if you even suggested it, they would laugh at you and tell you that you are wrong. Unless people actually do therapy, or are just really aware of themselves, most of their behavior is reflexive, unconscious. They do not think through or process what is going on with them."

Maggie continued, "Most people have no reason to look at what they do and say because they create a rationale in their minds for why they do what they do and say what they say. For example, your mother has created a rationale for her treatment of you by saying you are an 'instigator.' This way she can simply punish you and not see her two other children as anything less than perfect."

"Holy cow, this is a whole new way of looking at things!" I felt excited as I listened to Maggie. "I feel like my head is spinning. It's like looking at my mom and family from a different angle or something. I can sort of imagine them on a stage, and I'm in the audience looking at them. This is fascinating, Maggie."

"I will say this over and over to you, Samantha. Your family does not even know that this is happening. They are all stuck in their own realities—a reality created when they were children and then reinforced as they got older. For example, you said that your grandma and grandpa hated each other when he was alive. Did he drink like your dad? That would certainly have had an impact on your mother."

Maggie continued, "Whatever their relationship was—it helped create the woman your mother is today. Don't misunderstand me, Samantha, I am not saying that she is a bad person; I'm saying that she is an unaware person. Until you started therapy, you were an unaware person. Most of us live our whole lives totally unaware of the unconscious 'stuff' going on inside us every day."

Maggie stressed the point again. "Haven't you ever said or done something and later thought, 'Now, why did I do that?' It's almost as if someone else did it. Well, that is an example of being 'unaware.' It also explains what happens—when those 'parts' we talk about—act without supervision of the adult. They are like kids acting out. As I've said before the adult pays the price—it has to clean up the mess. That's why therapy is so important and why when you learn these skills, you feel so much more in control of your life."

"You also mentioned that your mom talks to you about your dad drinking. I don't know if she ever talked to him about it, but if she did, it obviously didn't do any good. Can you imagine how angry you would be if someone you loved just didn't listen to you? Here again we see a good reason for your mom to be angry, but the anger isn't being addressed or resolved. That anger has to go somewhere, Samantha. I think you hit it right when you said you thought it 'leaked' on to you kids and especially on to you."

"The fact that your father was not engaged with the daily activities of the family, leaving your mother to cope with everything, is another good reason for her anger. Again, we have no way of knowing whether she addressed any of these things with him, but we know that his behavior has not changed. I don't know about you, but I'd be plenty angry about that. The fact that they are so involved in the church may make it harder for your mother to get her needs met. Often, we believe we have to present the face of the 'perfect family' in social situations, especially in a church where we are prominent figures. When in reality, life is far from perfect."

"Oh, my God! This seems so right. I'm thinking you had a camcorder in my house all these years. It's like you know my family, Maggie." I was amazed and a little overwhelmed at how lots of things seemed to be falling into place.

Maggie continued, "People who live double lives, as it were, often feel very angry—mostly because there is no way for them to get their feelings validated. They simply can't tell anyone how bad it is because they do not want to be seen as less than perfect. Even the wife who has an alcoholic husband believes that people will wonder what was wrong with her that she chose him. In the case of your mom and dad, there was a pregnancy so it has to look happy at home because of the awkward beginning. She couldn't let the gossips be right—that the marriage might have been a mistake. So she lives a 'life of quiet desperation,' as Henry David Thoreau said."

"And on another subject, God only knows what the issues are between your mother and your grandmother, but I'm sure there is enough between them to fill a book. All I'm saying is that your grandmother and your mother are angry women, and your father is an angry man. He's probably drinking to medicate those feelings."

"I can't really say that I've ever seen my dad show *any* emotion. Well, he does say that he feels proud of Brian. I guess I've always felt closer to my dad because he never attacked me the way that my mom did."

Maggie responded thoughtfully. "It's easy to target the parent who was very verbal and who interacted a lot with you as 'the problem.' It is not as easy to figure out your own emotions about a parent when that parent has been somewhat absent. Your dad took on a lot of responsibility at a really young age when he and your mother got pregnant. You just have no way of knowing what kind of dreams he may have had, which were dashed when he found out about the pregnancy. You know for sure that while he has been financially responsible, he has not been very present in your life or anyone else's, including your mother's. Your father seems to have shut down and uses alcohol to numb whatever feelings he may have about his life."

"You said that your father's parents are not really part of the picture. Do you have any idea why? Maybe the answer to that question is another reason why your dad is angry. All I know <u>for sure is that you are surrounded by people who do not want to deal with their feelings,</u> and it's my job to teach you the skills to navigate these treacherous waters without getting dragged down yourself. Are you totally overwhelmed?" Maggie was looking at me with concern.

I was more amazed than overwhelmed. "Holy cow, that's a lot of information about where all the anger in my house may have originated." It seemed to me like she was 'right on' and it was a little overwhelming. *How had she gotten all that from that first session?* I thought again about the puzzle. It seemed like a lot more pieces had just been added to it, and it was coming together. The picture seemed to be getting clearer.

"I feel better when you explain about the anger that my parents might have for their parents and for each other, because now I can see that it wasn't about me at all. I can see that I was just 'handy.' I wasn't what they wanted. Not that they were really obvious about it, but they did treat me differently. It's amazing! I just flashed back to a situation that lets me know I'm not crazy. They really did treat me differently, Maggie."

"Tell me about it."

"I just flashed back to a night that Sarah came by the house to pick me up for a basketball game. Brian was junior varsity so he was long gone, their game was first. Kay was a cheerleader, so she also had already left for the game with Mom's blessing. I couldn't leave until I had completed the list of chores my mom had prepared. Sarah and I worked until 8:00 that night to get all the chores done. If I'd had to do them myself, I would have missed the whole varsity game instead of just half of it." I was starting to feel the anger rise in my throat as I talked about that night.

"Now there is an event I could journal about. I feel really angry when I think about it." The angry feelings were as strong now as they probably were that night.

"This is actually quite convenient," Maggie said. "I wanted to 'up the ante' on the anger work today, anyway."

"You wanted to what?" I was totally confused.

"Well, writing about your anger and addressing the person directly was a very good beginning. You got used to writing, 'When I think about…I feel angry, Mom.' That is the way to start. Now I want you to take it to another level." Maggie walked over to the couch and picked up a pillow. She handed it to me. She also picked one up for herself. She sat back down in her chair facing me with the pillow in her lap. "I want you to try visualizing your mother sitting on the couch. I want you to say these words out loud, 'I am so angry at you, Mom.'"

My first thought was, *This will be easy! I've been writing those words for a couple of weeks now.* Well, it turned out *not* to be that easy. Nothing would come out of my mouth. I could see my mom on the couch and, of course, I was four years old again. *Damn!* The tears were already beginning to sting behind my eyes.

Maggie saw what had happened and reminded me of the story I had been telling. She offered, "Try saying, 'When I think about the list of chores you gave me, I feel angry.' By the way, Samantha, it's also okay to say, 'I can cry and still be angry.' You are not weak just because you cry."

I took a deep breath and started. "You know what Mom? I'm angry at you. I am so angry at you! Why did I get the fucking lists and Kay get to go off with no chores to do? Why, Mom? I know I'm crying! I have a right to cry! I can cry and still be angry! I hate you, Mom! I hate you!" I started to cry so hard I couldn't talk any more and just hid my face in the pillow I had just been hitting. *I was I hitting a pillow? Holy shit, I must have looked really stupid!*

Again, Maggie simply sat with me while I cried, supporting my feelings and telling me that it was okay to have feelings, any feeling, sad or angry. When I finished crying, I blew my nose and leaned back in my chair. "Wow, what just happened? I feel like the weight of the world is off my shoulders."

"Well", Maggie said, "you just got rid of a lot of angry and sad energy that you have been holding in for a long time. I'm sure you are aware that as you were telling your mom how angry you were, you were also hitting that pillow in your lap. It's very common for people to do that. That's why I gave you the pillow first. Remember what I said about it not being okay to hurt people or things with your anger—including yourself. That's why I put the pillow on your lap. I didn't want you to hit your legs."

"This exercise is exactly what I meant by 'upping the ante.' Instead of just writing your anger, I want you to 'do' your anger. I want you to visualize the person with whom you are angry and say the words to them. Use a pillow like you just did so that you aren't hitting yourself or walls—that was a joke. I know you won't do that."

Maggie modeled for me how to hit the pillows. "You can sit in a chair with pillows in your lap protecting your legs or you can sit on the floor with several pillows in front of you. You did it naturally by yourself and, you did it perfectly. Just keep it up. I'll give you a handout so that you can see the steps you just went through." (The handout on anger work that Maggie gives Samantha is found in Appendix V.)

"Doing this helps you to get this anger out and deal with it. Remember what I said: <u>It is NOT okay to say these things directly to people.</u> You need to do this anger work in the privacy of your home—in your closet, if need be, when no one is home. It's also okay to do this in your parked car at lunch. Just don't let this Teenager talk directly to people. She's too much for them. And besides, she just gets you in trouble. She only sees one part of the picture. You, as the Adult Samantha, see the whole picture. Just because you see the whole picture, doesn't mean that she can't talk to you about what she sees. Sometimes you really do need all her information to process a situation correctly."

"When I talk about these 'parts,' Samantha, that is all they are—different parts of you. They all have information for you. Think of them as little cameras in your head taking snapshots of the events of your life. Each part has a lens that is a little different from the others. These snapshots just get filed away. Some are in the front of the file because these particular snapshots were of really important events—events that caused these various parts to feel extremely frightened, sad, or angry. Whenever something happens today that looks anything like those 'priority snapshots,' the parts are engaged. These parts aren't stupid. They are just immature."

"Have you ever just had a gut feeling about something and it turned out to be right, even though your rational mind could find nothing wrong with the situation? That was because one or more of these sub-personalities was telling you—'I have a snapshot of this from before—Look out!'"

"Again, I know I'm giving you a lot of information. I want you to do the anger work like you did it here today. As always, I wish that you had some support for doing this work. If Sarah is willing to sit with you, it would be wonderful. If she can't, that's okay. You obviously are able to do this on your own. I'm so glad that you had Sarah and her grandmother as models of healthy behavior when you were growing up. Whether you know it or not, you were taking snapshots of them. You are drawing on those now to support yourself through this work. You are a very strong woman, Samantha. I'm pleased that I have the opportunity to work with you."

"The final step to bring closure to the anger work is to address the person you are angry with as an adult. If mom were sitting in that chair right now, what would you say to her about that night?"

"Well, Maggie, I guess I would just say, 'Mom, I'm angry! That was really unfair of you. Don't ever treat me that way again.' How was that? It felt good to say it—even though I know I'd probably never say it to her face."

"That's the beauty of this work. You never have to say a word to her if you don't want to and yet you are 'done' with that event. The only one with undealt with feelings is your mother."

"Wow! This is really pretty wonderful! I feel ten years younger."

"Great! Now for some sobering news, you do realize that we only have two more sessions that are paid for by your insurance, don't you? We can continue on a sliding fee scale or try to wrap it up in the next two sessions. I think we should leave at least two weeks between now and the next session, maybe three weeks. How does that sound to you?"

"Maggie, I've learned so much. I think I'll be fine at the end of the six sessions. Let's go two weeks before we meet again. That will give me plenty of time to work on this anger stuff. This is really weird. I tell Sarah everything, and I'm not sure exactly how to broach the subject of this session. I'll do it though. It felt too good not to keep doing it."

"I'm also assuming that you do a lot of anger work at first and then not so much, right?" If I understood what Maggie was saying, I would work on the old issues I had saved in the file drawer and then I would be done with them.

Maggie looked at me with her kind eyes. "I wish it were that easy. Yes, you are right that you will do a lot of anger work at first. You will find that pretty soon you aren't as angry as you used to be. In your case, Samantha, I think you'll know when you find that you don't swear so much. Things will still happen that trigger your anger. When you are triggered, do your anger work."

"What you will find," she continued, "is that half the time you are not angry about what you thought you were angry about. Again, an example might help here. I had some problems with one of my professors in college. He made what I thought were unreasonable demands on me. I got so angry. A part of me wanted to just tell him where to go—and it was not a good place, I might add." She said, laughing. "My therapist had me do my anger work. As I was saying to my professor, 'When you make unreasonable demands, I feel angry,' my dad's face showed up instead of my professor's. I was then able to get angry at my dad, telling him how unreasonable he had been with me as a child and how angry I was about it. After I got clear about whom the real target of my anger was and why I was *so* angry, I was then able to go to my professor as an adult woman and talk through our differences."

"There is magic in this work. The magic, Samantha, is that the professor became one of my absolute favorites. He did demand a lot, but he pulled the best from me in ways no one else could have. If I hadn't done the work, I would have made a terrible mistake. He was a hard man but a good man. It was my dad who was the jerk and deserved all that anger. If I hadn't done the work, I might not be sitting here now. My professor believed in me. He encouraged me because he saw something no one else saw. He saw my ability, my potential. He saw the good in me that I was not able to see because of my childhood. I wouldn't be sitting here if it hadn't been for his vision of who I could become."

"Things like that will happen all the time. As long as you are willing to go some place by yourself and do your anger work, the adult in you will keep you on the right path.

As I said before, it's wise to keep that Teenager in check. She can get you into a lot of trouble. And, unfortunately, it's the adult who has to clean up her messes."

"Any questions? No. Okay! Call me if you have any difficulties over the next two weeks." Maggie stood up.

"Thanks, Maggie. It helps so much just to talk about all this stuff and get a new perspective. Sometimes it's painful, but I always end up feeling better after I see you—exhausted, but better. This should be a long but very interesting two weeks."

chapter 9

"Hi, Mom." It had been a week since my therapy session. I had done so much anger work that I was hoarse. It had been a really good week for me, and I felt good, lighter. I even decided to "face my demons" and go see the folks. It was sort of worth it to see the look on my mom's face when I walked through the door unannounced.

"Well, to what do we owe this honor? The queen has finally decided to honor us with her presence. I would think you'd be ashamed to show your face after standing us up last weekend." She sniped at me. My mother was in rare form, it seemed.

"Mom, I did call to tell you that I wasn't coming. What more do you want?"

"Oh, leave her alone, Susan." Grandma came rushing up to give me a big hug. "What are you up to, honey? Are you losing weight? Susan, get her some of that chocolate cake you made. She's way too skinny. Come on, let's go in the kitchen."

Never one to turn down chocolate cake, Grandma and I headed for the kitchen with Mom following. There was no way she was going to leave me alone with Grandma for a minute.

"Actually, I'm running away from home for a little while. Sarah and Tim and all his friends are moving him in today. There were so many of them that I was just in the way. I thought I'd drive over here and just check in with you. How's everything?" It felt good to be here. It smelled good here. I didn't feel angry. I was able to just see my mom and how her life may not have turned out exactly as she might have wanted it to. I saw how Grandma rubbed her the wrong way, but she put up with it because Grandma was her mom. What else could she do? I was floating on a cloud of self-awareness and it felt great!

The cake was incredible—as usual. *Man, Mom can bake a cake!* I started cutting a second piece.

"Samantha, you have to watch what you eat! You'll look like a pig if you keep that up."

"No, I won't, Mom. I work out five days a week. I'm fine. Nobody bakes or cooks like you. I'm eating this." I continued eating to the sound of my mother huffing and puffing around in the kitchen. *Maybe this isn't going to be as easy as I thought.* Grandma had already headed back to the living room when things started to heat up between me and Mom. *What a chicken!*

Mom interrupted my thoughts with, "Tim is moving in with you and Sarah? Well, I think it's awful. It's sinful. What is it with you young people now days? It's just not right to live together before marriage. It goes against everything the church teaches."

My mom and her church teachings, not my favorite rant, but one I was used to. It was interesting to me that she couldn't accept my compliment but instead turned the topic to something that was going to be uncomfortable for everyone. *Hmmm.*

"Like you have any room to talk about what the church teaches," Grandma yelled from the living room. She had hit the ball out of the park on that one.

My mother deflated like a balloon that had just been stuck with a pin. I couldn't handle the pain in her eyes—Sammy to the rescue, as usual. "Come on, Mom. Let's run over to the mall. Do you want to come, Grandma?" I knew she wouldn't so it was safe to ask. "Grab your purse, Mom." Grandma was watching one of the old movies they play 24/7 for the old folks. She seemed to have disappeared into the couch as Mom and I headed out the door.

I wanted to set the parameters of the visit early. "I don't have much time. I don't want to be gone too long. Tim's buying pizza for all the movers and I don't want to miss that even though I haven't helped much. I just wanted to see you—see how you are doing. I haven't been over for a while. I know, I know, don't start on me not coming last weekend." Mom seemed older to me for some reason.

As I was clearing off the front seat, my mother stood waiting with her hands on her hips. She had 'the look' on her face. As she climbed in the car, she said, "This car is a mess. Don't you ever clean it?"

Is it possible to feel your own blood pressure rising? *Oh my God! I am already triggered and we haven't even pulled out of the driveway!* Once on the street, I worked at calming myself, trying to breathe. It worked for a couple minutes anyway.

"Your father did a lousy job of teaching you to drive. Why do you keep weaving in and out of traffic? Have you called your sister or brother lately? Just asking—I know it's none of my business." Mom could probably go on for hours, but I was reaching my limit. How can things go this bad, this fast? It was unbelievable! Her voice was starting to sound like nails on a chalkboard in my head.

Okay, I've had it! I was talking to myself while Mom droned on. I was disappointed in myself, and at the same time I felt good that I knew when I'd had enough. "You know what? I'm really thirsty. Let's just stop and get a Coke, and I'll take you back home. Does that work for you? I really am feeling guilty about not helping with the move." I was struggling to come up with some way out of this mess. I knew I couldn't keep my cool much longer. I didn't want to blow up on her. She didn't deserve it. Perhaps this experiment had been a little premature.

"I don't really care what you do, Samantha. I certainly don't want a Coke. You know how bad all that caffeine is for you. I know it doesn't matter what I say. You'll do what you want anyway. You always have." After a heavy sigh loud enough to make me wonder if she had pneumonia, she continued. "I just can't believe that you would be a party to someone living in sin. Of course, all of you young people are doing it these days. You aren't, but that's only because you can't find anyone who will put up with you. I'm certainly glad that your sister Kay was a virgin when she got married."

I sort of choked. I thought I was going to bite my tongue off. Kay was a virgin until she was about 15. She met Mike, and they were doing it every chance they got.

Mike was older and knew enough to use condoms, or they would have been in the same boat Mom and Grandma had found themselves. Kay certainly never took any precautions. I started to do my deep breathing. I was praying that I wasn't going to hyperventilate.

"What are you doing?" My mother was obviously perplexed by my breathing ritual.

"Oh, nothing," I answered as calmly as I could. Thankfully, the woman at the drive-through got my Coke quickly, and we headed home. "I'm taking Yoga. I really love it. I think it helps me drive better."

"Well, it doesn't." Mom always had an opinion, and of course it was always negative.

"Are you happy, Mom?" It was out of my mouth before I could stop myself. *Was I nuts?*

"Of course, I'm happy. What a strange thing to ask me. Kay told me that you were in therapy. This must be some kind of an assignment or something. Well, you can tell that shrink of yours that I'm happy. We're all happy. The only one who's not happy seems to be you. So you just keep going to see this person until you're happy. Then, maybe when you deign to come by the house to see us you'll be easier to get along with. *Really,* am *I* happy? What a silly question. I hope you find what you are looking for, Samantha. I personally think that you would have a better chance finding what you want in church, but if you want to pursue this silly therapy thing, more power to you. Here we are. Just let me off in front. This car is a moving garbage can. I guess I know what to give you for Christmas—coupons for that car wash down the street." And she was gone.

It felt like she had sucked all the air out of the car as she slammed the door. "I can breathe." I was taking in big gulps of air. "I can breathe. I can do this—breathe in to the count of four, out to the count of four. I can interact with my mother and not die. Here I am driving my car. I survived. Breathe in—1, 2, 3, 4. Breathe out—1, 2, 3, 4. Well, so much for confronting my mother's behavior in a healthy way. Guess I'll save that for another day." What a nightmare that had turned into.

I couldn't decide if I felt more sad or more angry. I decided I had better stop to regroup before I went home, especially with a house full of strangers. Maybe I'd go to the park by our house and try to settle myself. I was now carrying a pillow in the car—part of the garbage mom had pointed out. I found it convenient to smash the pillow when I was particularly angry in traffic. It really worked.

Good, the park was deserted. I parked Lizzie and headed for a spot that Sarah and I often visited when Shiloh needed to run or we needed to just get out of the apartment. I saw someone as I got closer. "Shit," I muttered under my breath. "Someone's here." I turned to walk back to the car when Shiloh came bounding up to me.

"Sammy," Sarah yelled. "What are you doing here?"

"If I told you, you wouldn't believe it." I think she could tell how upset I was.

"What happened?" The look on her face was pure love and concern. Sarah was so sweet to me. I can handle almost anything but sweetness. People being nice to me is not something I had experienced much as a child. When people are nice to me, it always brings me to the verge of tears. "Sit down, tell me about it," she said.

"I tried to talk to my mom. Obviously, it didn't work. God, Sarah, why does it have to be so difficult with her? All I want is to have a decent conversation. I just want us to talk like normal people. <u>I just want</u> her to be nice to me." As I said those words, the tears started. I cried and cried, and Sarah just sat with me. It was so good to feel her with me without any advice or criticism.

It took a while until I finally calmed down. "You know what? Now I feel angry. Do you mind if I do the anger work that Maggie taught me to do? It seems a little weird, but you'll understand when you see it."

Sarah looked quizzical. "What are you talking about, Sammy? You haven't said anything about anger work to me."

"I haven't had time. Things have been moving like greased lightening at our house, in case you haven't noticed. We haven't had time to exchange more than 'Hi' and 'Goodbye', much less explain this whole thing. Want to hear about it now?"

"Sure, the guys are watching football at home. They got done moving stuff and just decided to hang 'til the football game was over. Tim is calling for pizza when the game is in the final minutes so we need to be home soon. Oh well, forget that. We all know the last football minute takes at least a half an hour or so. How long will this take?" She looked quizzical.

"It doesn't take long at all. I'll be right back." I took off running for the car to grab my pillow. I was winded when I got back but still feeling angry. I told Sarah to have a seat. "This is anger work. I'm going to visualize my mother right now and tell her how angry I am at her."

"Well, I'm for this. I've been wishing you would do this for years. Of course, I was hoping you would tell her to her face, but this is better than nothing." Sarah was clearly a willing participant.

"I am so angry at you, Mom! You basically just called me a slob, a sinner, and a fat pig, and I'm angry about that. I am so mad at you." As I said the words, I hit the pillow just like I had done many times last week. I let it all out. I yelled at my mom for all the times she had called me names or belittled me. Sarah just sat with me while I did the anger work. She never said a word. She supported me just as Maggie had done. When I was finished, I just sat back and took a few deep breaths. "That feels great. It's really nice to get it out right after something happens. I've been working on old stuff all week, but this feels really good."

"Wow! That was amazing! I have never seen you angry like that before. It's nothing like when you are throwing things and stomping around the apartment. This isn't scary. Are you okay?" Sarah was looking at me like she had never really seen me before. As usual, she was just present, not critical. "Tell me more about the 'anger work' thing the therapist has you doing. You were amazing."

As I told Sarah about anger work, the way Maggie had explained it to me; I could see the interest in her eyes. It certainly looked like I had peaked her curiosity.

"This sounds like a really good idea. And you say that you feel way better after you do it?" Sarah seemed a little incredulous.

"I really do. I feel like I'm getting rid of something. I also feel way more powerful. It's kind of weird how it works—but it works!" I could see that I really didn't have to sell Sarah on this. She was kind of kneading the pillow, and I could almost see her itching to hit it.

"So, who are you angry at right now, Sarah?" I could see that she wanted to punch that pillow just like she had seen me hit it. I was shocked when she started to punch the pillow and yell at MY mom.

"Mrs. Daley, you are such a bitch. I've watched you attack Samantha for years. You are so mean to her, and I'm mad at you for that. I love her! She's my friend, and you are so mean to her. Stop it! Stop it! Stop it!" Sarah leaned back. "Man, this does feel good!" She looked at me like a little kid who was very pleased with herself. "How'd I do?" She asked.

I just burst into tears. *What the heck?* I just cried and cried. I couldn't stop. Sarah was rubbing my back.

"I'm so sorry, Sam. I didn't mean to upset you. I've just been so mad at your mom for so long. Oh, God, I'm so sorry. I shouldn't have said all that in front of you. Oh Sam, please stop crying! I won't say another word about your mom, ever. Please, please forgive me, Sam. You know that I wouldn't hurt you for the world!"

When I could stop sobbing and catch my breath, I put my arms around Sarah and gave her a big hug. "Sarah, I'm not upset because you yelled at my mom. Just the opposite, I felt protected by you. I've never had anybody speak up for me. It just felt so good. I know it was just pretend, but it still felt fabulous! I just couldn't control myself. I'm sorry I made you feel bad. What you did was so nice. Thank you so much." I felt loved and cared for. I felt validated and protected. What a wonderful feeling!

"I think I understand now why Maggie says that I should do this with you first. It is so that I have a model for my adult to follow. I think she wants me to be able to do what you just did. She wants me to protect myself the way you just did. I'm telling you, my friend, you can do anger work at my mom any time you want." I was euphoric. I started laughing, almost as hard as I'd cried. What a wonderful way to end the awful time I had just spent with my mom.

I gave Sarah a big hug as we stood up. "You are the best, my friend." We both headed for our cars. As we approached the parking lot, Shiloh started doing her spinning in circles thing. She finally decided she was going to ride home with me. Sarah took off for her car at the other end of the parking lot. She called over her shoulder, "I forgot to tell you. Lon called."

"Thanks," I yelled. *Wonder what he wants now.* Lon was an on-again, off-again boyfriend. Sarah didn't like him. She thought he used me. Oh well, being 'used' is not always a bad thing—Lon is a hunk!

chapter 10

I COULDN'T BELIEVE how fast the time had gone since my last session with Maggie. I told her about the anger work I had done. Her eyes actually filled with tears when I told her about the work I had done with Sarah at the park. "I still feel like I'm on a roller coaster, but a good one now. I really do have way more ups than downs. I feel bad that I couldn't talk to my mom better. Wow, I got triggered really, really bad. I was gone. There was no adult at home at all—well maybe I stayed present for a few minutes."

Maggie was all over that statement. "Samantha, you did a wonderful job. It is really hard to get and maintain good boundaries with your parents, especially mothers. She carried you inside her body and nursed you. There was no boundary at that point in time. She is only doing what she has done all your life. In her mind, your life is her life. It's really hard for parents to let go of children. You are the one who has to 'grow up.' She is not willingly going to let any of you change into equal-power adults."

Maggie continued, "This doesn't make her a bad person. In fact, I'd say she is acting pretty normal. Most people go through this with their parents. It's called differentiation. Look at your mom and grandma. They are still connected in an unhealthy, unequal relationship. They will probably never individuate—truly be separate individuals. It is really a very difficult process for all involved. The healthier the parents are, the easier the process of differentiation is for the young person."

"Now, let's go back over all of your accomplishments, Samantha. You did a lot of anger work. You were able to do your breathing exercises even when you were in very difficult situations. You kept up with your journaling. That is a lot. You have more to be proud about than you have to be disappointed about. Good work."

"But I really failed with Mom." I felt so bad about how I had handled that situation.

"Did you, Samantha?" Maggie probed. "It sounds to me like you got to say a couple of things that you wanted to say. It just didn't go the way that you had wanted it to go. You wanted to have the kind of talk with your mom that you have with Sarah. Samantha, don't you think you are expecting a little too much from your mom? I bet she has never in her life had a talk like you are imagining—with anyone. If you are going to move in the direction of a healthy relationship, it will take time—a long time. You are the one who is going to have to be patient."

"I'm not saying that you should continue to take her criticism. You and I will work out some ways to confront her negativity, but that is different than having a real relationship. Remember that I said in the beginning it takes two adults to have a relationship. You both have to be able to identify what you are feeling and what you need. Then you have to be able to negotiate so that both of you get your needs met. Well, your mom's not able to do those things. You are half her age, and you are struggling to get in touch with those feelings. You can't expect her to overcome years of old messages that 'her needs are not important' quickly. I don't know if she can ever get in touch with her feelings and needs. She was programmed—like you have been—to believe that it is selfish to even have needs."

Maggie looked at me to see if I understood her. "You both have all the time you need, Samantha. <u>You'll come to an understanding of yourself and of your mother, and then you'll choose what kind of a relationship you want to be in with her.</u>"

Something in the way Maggie said those words gave me hope. I didn't know for sure what I was even hopeful about. I just felt more in control of the direction my relationship with Mom would go.

"Let's talk about 'I' messages." Maggie was clearly ready to move on to more skills training. "Your mother is always telling you who you are. Right?"

"Yes, that was why I got so angry. She was telling me that I don't know how to drive, keep my car clean, how to eat, and on and on *ad nauseum*. I get so sick of hearing how bad I am or how wrong I am." I could feel the anger rising, but not like it had in the past. Maybe this 'anger' work thing did help.

"No one likes to be told who they are," Maggie continued. "Usually, we know our faults pretty well; no one needs to remind us. I always say that if we were never criticized again, we've heard all we need to continue to walk the straight and narrow. We know the right thing to do, and most of us try to do that. So the question is, how do you confront that behavior in your mom?—very carefully!" Maggie laughed at her own joke. I liked her laugh. It was contagious. I laughed with her.

"All 'you statements' are attacks on your boundary. Essentially the person is telling you that she or he knows you better than you know yourself. If your mother says, 'You shouldn't eat so much,' she is telling you that you don't know yourself well enough to know when you have had enough to eat. Remember, your boundary is being able to say, 'I know me.' So the antidote to a 'you statement' is an 'I statement.' In the case of your mother telling you that you would get fat from eating that second piece of cake, you did it perfectly. You said, if I remember correctly, 'No, I won't. I work out five days a week.' Do you see that intuitively you used your knowledge of yourself and counteracted her attack?"

"Wow, you're right! I did! I can't believe it, but I did! I remember feeling really good when I said that, too. She didn't look stricken the way she did when Grandma attacked her either. She just started cleaning the kitchen—she did do quite a bit of 'harrumphing' though. The amazing thing is that she shut up about the food thing for a while. I think I get what you are saying." I felt better knowing that I hadn't failed completely in that encounter with my mom.

"You were successful on several levels, Samantha." Maggie was clearly in cheerleader mode today. "You didn't engage with your mother when you knew there was no point. When she attacked Tim and Sarah about living together; and when she told you that you could solve your problems by going to church—you just didn't engage.

Not on page

That was a really healthy thing to do. You weren't going to win that one. Your mother has her beliefs, and they work for her. She doesn't understand that they might not work for you. You are not going to convince her that you are different. You solve your problems differently than she does. You have a right to solve your problems any way that you want to solve them. She doesn't have a right to tell you how to solve your problems, but she doesn't see that. You are never going to convince her of it either. You are better off just letting her say her piece and moving on. You did a good job listening to her."

"I felt like I was just being a chicken." I couldn't let myself hear that I might have done a good job when it felt like I just ran.

"Ask yourself, 'What would have happened if I had engaged with my mom on this issue?' If the answer is, 'It would have turned into a screaming match,' then you did the right thing by letting her have her say. You know where she stands on the issue, and it's a done deal. You don't have to agree, and you don't have to convince her she is wrong—you never will. You need to learn that there are just some hills that aren't worth climbing. You confronted her on the cake issue—and won, I might add. You let the religion thing go. Good work!" I could see that Maggie was actually feeling happy about my accomplishments.

"Why is it so hard for me to see the good? You just gave me several compliments, and I tried to get you to focus on what I had done wrong. You know, I saw my mom do that, too. Is it possible to inherit that?"

Maggie laughed again. "No, Samantha, you didn't inherit it. You did grow up around your mom, who can't accept a compliment so she modeled that behavior for you. You also grew up in a house where people were very negative. Your dad is just sort of out of it. He doesn't really engage at all, and your mom is really critical, especially of you. So you picked up the message that you are wrong or bad; and when someone says something nice, it feels uncomfortable so you just dismiss it. That's why Sarah's sweetness 'gets' to you. It's not something that you are familiar with so you get a little overwhelmed by it."

"Maggie, can I tell you something that I've never told anyone?"

"Of course, Samantha, you can tell me anything. That is what this 'therapy thing' is all about. What is it?"

"When Sarah, or anyone else for that matter, is nice to me, it makes my heart hurt." I was starting to cry as I said the words. "Am I weird, Maggie? What's wrong with me?"

"Samantha, you aren't weird. That is an experience that you share with many people. When you come out of a really critical, negative environment, it is normal to feel discomfort when people are kind. The pain in your heart just means that their words or deeds got to you. That's a good thing. You deserve to have people be kind to you."

"So from now on, when people are giving you a compliment or being nice to you, I want you to take a really deep breath. I call it, 'breathing in the good.' You know what you do when you walk in to a bakery, or into your mother's kitchen, you take a deep breath to smell the good food. Well, I want you to do the same thing with good words. If you forget to do it, I want you to ask people to repeat what they have said. You can go back a day or two later and say, 'Hey, you gave me a compliment and I didn't really hear it.

Would you repeat what you said so that I can hear it this time?' I can see by the look on your face, Samantha, that you think I'm crazy, but it works. You have to *learn* to hear the good. Like any other skill, it takes practice."

As Maggie talked, I remembered that line in the movie, *Pretty Woman*, 'Why is it always easier to believe the bad things about yourself?' I repeated that line to Maggie.

"You resonated with that line because that was your reality, Samantha. It doesn't have to remain your reality. You are a wonderful, sweet, bright, funny young woman. There is so much that is good about you. It is time that you begin to see who you really are instead of believing the messages you've been given about who you are. It is the difference between looking in a mirror and seeing the image of the real you, and looking at a painting of yourself. Your parents, siblings, church, and community, among others, painted a picture of who you were *supposed to be* for them. It never felt right to you because it wasn't you. Now you are looking in a mirror, and the real you is smiling back at you. I think you are becoming more and more comfortable with the real Samantha Daley that you see in that mirror. I know I like what I see." I could feel the acceptance and support in Maggie's voice.

"I will continue to work on hearing the good things that people say to me, Maggie. Gee, at work people are wonderful to me. I actually get a lot of praise at work. I think I am pretty much able to hear it, too. I guess what I want is to be able to get that affirmation and love and acceptance from my family. Are you saying that I will never get what I want from them?" I felt a kind of loneliness as I said the words.

"I'm not saying that, Samantha. I don't know what your family will be able to give you. You just need to start slow. Don't have big expectations, and then you won't have big disappointments. Think small. What are little things that you can ask for that maybe Mom or Dad can give you. Perhaps you could begin by telling Dad that you need some time alone with him. I'm suggesting that you start with your dad, because he appears to be pretty low-key. I can't imagine him getting upset by that request or saying anything negative—I've been wrong before, so be prepared."

"Let me give you an example, Samantha. I tried to connect with my father. It didn't go very well at all, at first. I asked him to tell me that he loved me. He responded by yelling at me. He yelled something like, 'Of course I love you. I put a roof over your head and fed you didn't I?' Okay, I did get the words, 'I love you.' Unfortunately, the words were delivered in such a way that it was very hard for me to hear them."

"Remember, I told you I get triggered by loud, male voices. I had to do work similar to what you reported doing when your mother got out of the car. I just kept reminding myself to breathe and to focus on him saying, 'Of course, I love you.' It was hard work, but I was finally able to 'get' that he loved me. That was my goal, to hear that he loved me. If I had let the delivery get in the way, I would never have been able to 'let in' the words."

"Do I wish it would have all gone down differently? Of course. I wanted him to give me a big hug, laugh and say something like, 'Of course I love you. Who wouldn't love a daughter as wonderful as you are?' He couldn't do that. No one had ever done that for him, so he just didn't have the vocabulary or the ability to do it. That is sad for both of us. I hope that your dad will handle the situation differently than mine did. What's important is that you begin reaching out as an adult woman. You may or may not get your needs met with your dad. You have to remember that you will *never* get them met if you don't try."

"As far as your mom is concerned, again think small," Maggie continued. "You did such a great job when she was sarcastic with you about eating. Take those opportunities to be healthy with her every time you get a chance."

"But, Maggie, I don't seem to know that those things are happening until after they are over. I'll be driving home, or it will be two days later, and I will think to myself, 'She got me again.' How do I catch it in the moment? That really did feel good to do it right when it happened."

Maggie was excited. "Remember what we talked about in your first session? You know when someone has 'gotten to you' by the way your body reacts. I think you said that it felt like someone had punched you in the gut. That's your cue. If you feel that twinge in your gut while at your mom's, just tune her out a minute, and see what she said or did that caused the reaction. When you get clear, take a deep breath and make your 'I statement' back to her. You've already done it once. You can do this. When you get in touch with your feelings—and consequently your needs—and come from your core knowledge of yourself, you are truly in your power. It is pretty hard for your mother to argue with that. Does this make sense to you?"

"Totally!" I think I was as excited as Maggie. "I really do get what you are saying. I do know that when people say things that trigger me, I feel it first in my gut. I also think that

I resort to the fight or flight breathing you talked about. Those will both be my cues. Actually you said I should take a deep breath first so that will help get my 'adult' breathing started. This is really amazing stuff! And what you are saying is that the skills I'm learning work with everyone, right? I mean I do all these same things no matter who triggers me."

"You are absolutely right, Samantha. The skills sound easy, get in touch with your feelings, express them. Get in touch with your needs, express them. Listen to and validate others, and finally, negotiate so both parties get their needs met. It all sounds easy, but these are the hardest things you'll ever do because you've been trained to *not* know yourself. And you have learned to start defending yourself—in your head—while you try to listen to others, rather than *really listening* to them. It is hard, but it is also really worth the time and trouble to learn all this. As I said before, it is like learning a foreign language."

"Do you want to 'role play' a scenario with your mom so that you have some practice?" Maggie asked.

"Sure, how do we do that?" This seemed a little silly, but I knew that if I practiced once, maybe it would be easier when I actually had to deal with my mom.

"Well, I'll just play your mom, Samantha. You focus on tuning into your feelings and using 'I statements.' Here goes."

"Samantha, this car is a mess. What is your problem? Why can't you do a simple thing like keep your car clean?" Maggie delivered a flawless performance.

"Uh…I don't know what to say." This was weird. I felt just like I feel when I'm with my mom. "Maggie, help!"

"Okay, Samantha, breathe. Remember, 'I statements'. How about something like, 'I'm different than you, Mom. You like a clean car. I like my 'stuff' all around me. I like my car this way."

"Well, I do like my car the way I keep it. But isn't that wrong? Shouldn't I *want* my car to be clean?" I was still feeling triggered and trapped.

"I'm serious now. You need to breathe." I could tell Maggie was concerned. "Who are you listening to when you get into the 'shoulds'? You are listening to the critic—more commonly known as your mother." That got a laugh from both of us. "You are breathing normally again. Let's do it again."

"Samantha, this car is a mess. Why can't you do a simple thing like keep your car clean?" Maggie sat back.

I took a deep breath—that would piss my mother off from the 'get go'. "Mom, I actually like my car like this. It's my traveling office. I like everything within easy reach. It doesn't bother me at all to have 'stuff' around me. I'm just different than you." I took another deep breath. "I did it!" I practically yelled at Maggie. "I felt strong and powerful. Yeah!"

"And you sounded strong and powerful," Maggie responded. "Just keep that up. It was perfect. If you know you are going to be seeing her, say some of those sentences out loud to yourself in the car as you drive. Put some of them in your journal. This is a new language remember. It's like learning the new vocabulary. Remember, all 'I statements.' It's no fair doing to her what she does to you."

"Are we going to do two weeks again? Or, since the next session is your last one, do you want to try three weeks?" Maggie asked.

"I can't believe it's my last session next time. I've learned so much. Let's do two weeks. I'll let you know if I want to continue when I see you. Thanks so much. You take care."

chapter 11

"WELL, WHAT ARE you going to do?" Sarah asked. She and I were in the park walking Shiloh. It seemed like we spent a lot of time walking Shiloh these days because it was the only way we got time alone now that Tim had moved in. She was talking about my indecisiveness about doing additional sessions with Maggie.

"I don't know. I am really feeling so much clearer about everything. I'm journaling, and I do 'anger work' when I need to. I seem to be maintaining really well. I can even handle Tim and 'the guys' when they show up unannounced to watch sports—is that all men want to do, by the way? Hey, who's the tall, dark-haired guy? I think his name is Brad. He's kind of cute." Tim had so many friends, it was hard to keep them all straight. This one kept looking at me though. He was different than the others. He actually put his beer cans in the recycle bin. Nice guy.

"Brad is one of Tim's partners. Tim is the computer geek end of the business; Brad is sales. He's cute, isn't he? And he's nice, too." Sarah was looking at me now—which is hard to do when you're walking side-by-side. Obviously she was trying to get a feel for what was going on with me regarding Brad.

"Yeah, I can believe he's in sales. The way he looks at me I'm pretty sure he wants to sell me something, and it has nothing to do with computers." We both laughed.

"I know Lon called again. Are you going out with him?" Sarah was never one to be subtle or beat around the bush.

"I know you hate Lon, Sarah. He's just such a hunk. When he shows up, he's really nice; and we have a lot of fun." I was feeling a little defensive. "I need to tell you that I'm feeling defensive, Sarah. It feels silly saying it but I'm trying to practice what Maggie taught me to do—tell you what I'm feeling. I can't do it with everyone, but I can do it with you. It feels good to be honest about what I'm feeling. I want to talk about Lon, but not if you are going to be angry at me about him." *Whew, that helped.* I took a deep breath. "I feel better. You can talk now." We both laughed.

Sarah continued. "Sam, I'm not angry about Lon. I'm angry *at* him. The key words in your sentence were 'when he's around.' He calls you when he's between girlfriends, and you know it. He doesn't want to settle down. He wants a good time. I think you deserve more than that. God, I'll never forget the time you found some other woman's makeup and lingerie in his bathroom and he told you they were his sister's. I feel really frustrated with you when you buy his bull. But, more than that, I'm just plain angry at him for being such a jerk with you"

"Bottom line, I care about you, Sam," Sarah continued. "If you want Lon, I'll be okay with that. And you know that's true. I don't have to like it, but I love you and nothing will come between the two of us. I feel better just saying all that. I guess this 'honesty thing' works both ways."

"So, back to my original question, are you going to do more sessions with Dr. DeWitt?"

"I don't think so. I could afford it if I thought I needed it, but I think I'm doing really well. I think I'm going to at least try to do it on my own. I've got so much stuff to practice. I'll be working on what I've learned for a year." As I said the words, I could feel that it was the right decision.

When we got out of the car in the parking lot, Shiloh jumped out before I could get her on her leash. She took off for the figure standing near our steps—Brad. "Oh great, we have company again tonight."

"Is that so bad?" Sarah asked.

"You are twinkling. You can't hide anything from me. I know you too well. Are you and Tim in on this together? Sarah, I'm just not ready to be thinking about some guy. I'm just starting to get healthy. I need to get to know myself first. That's a challenge in and of itself. Plus, I haven't tried being healthy with Lon. Give me a break, Sarah."

"You can't blame me for trying. It would be great if we were both involved with guys who were business partners. We'd be spending a lot of time together. I know it's silly, but I am so going to miss you when Tim and I move out. I know we both have to get our own lives. It's inevitable. You are my only family, besides Granny, and she's not going to be around forever." Sarah linked her arm in mine, and the two of us headed for the stairs.

"Your granny will outlive both of us. Didn't she just walk that 5K? I wish I had her energy." My attention shifted when we got to the stairs. "Hi, Brad. I see you found a friend. Which sport are you guys watching tonight? I'm so glad that we have cable *and* TIVO. It must make your life so much simpler."

"Samantha, did I detect a note of sarcasm in that?" Brad was smiling as he said it but seemed genuinely worried that he was crossing some line.

"No, Brad, I try not to use sarcasm any more. If I don't like something, I actually say it. I'm fine with you guys watching sports. It gives me time with Sarah and time for myself. We never watched that much TV before Tim moved in. We have our regulars that we TIVO, and that's about it. I'm glad you came over." I could feel the rightness of that statement, and I think it showed in my face. Brad gave me a squeeze before he took off up the stairs, taking them two at a time.

"You are right, Sarah. He's a nice guy."

As I opened the door, Tim yelled, "Sam, some guy named Lon called for you. I told him you'd be right back. Oh, and your mother called. She sounded upset."

"Shocker!" I muttered under my breath as I headed for my bedroom.

I paced my bedroom for a few minutes. If I'm going to talk to her, I need to breathe. I practiced my deep breathing—deep breath in, exhale out. I didn't want to talk to her until I felt really grounded. I lay down on my bed with my hand on my belly. 'Breathe until you feel your belly rise.' I could hear Maggie in my head. I could feel myself calming down. "I can do this." I said the words out loud to no one. It made me feel better; that's all that mattered. I sat down at my desk to dial the phone.

"Hi, Mom, what's up?"

"Who is this? Is that you, Sammy? I talk to you so seldom that I hardly recognize your voice anymore." Her voice was dripping with sarcasm.

I could feel my gut tighten. *Oh boy, here we go. Take a deep breath. She's already off and running.*

"Mom, I talked to you a few days ago." *Good, I made an 'I statement.' Breathe! Breathe!*

"Are you doing that crazy yoga thing? Could you do that some other time? It drives me crazy." Mom was clearly upset and getting more upset by the minute.

"What's wrong, Mom?" I tried to breathe more quietly—I knew for sure I wasn't going to stop the deep breathing.

"Brian has decided that he is going to move in with Amanda." As soon as she said the words, she was sobbing in earnest.

I just sat listening on the phone. "I hear you, Mom. It has to be hard for you." *Okay, who's talking? This can't be me. She drives me nuts and I'm being nice. Oh, my God, I'm being nice.* I loved it that I was able to do for my mom what I wanted and needed. And, I felt good doing it.

"What is that, 'therapy' talk?" Mom snapped at me.

"Mom, I was just trying to tell you that I understand." At that moment I saw the beginning of the train wreck in my head—and I was on the train. *No, wait. I can get off.*

"How could you understand? You aren't a mother. I don't know why I even bother to try to talk to you, Samantha. I should have just called Kay. She would understand."

"That sounds like a good idea, Mom. Why don't you call Kay?" *I did it! I got off the train!* "I'm sorry that you are so upset, Mom. Take care, and give Dad my love. Bye."

"I did it!" I actually tried to be nice to my mom. It didn't work, but who cares. I did it, and I felt good doing it. I was taking in big gulps of air. *This has got to get easier as I do it more. It has to!* I don't think my heart can stand this on a sustained basis. Every time I took one of my stands, my heart felt like it was beating so loudly, everyone around could hear it. I didn't really have any misgivings about doing this though. It was already getting easier with each new attempt at healthy communication. *Maybe it's time to try talking to my dad. Oh, my gosh, am I a glutton for punishment or what?* Before I could talk to him as an adult, I needed to clear up some of the old stuff that I was still harboring.

Over the next few days I did a lot of journaling and a lot of anger work. I decided that I wanted to try the experiment Maggie and I had discussed. I decided that I didn't want to risk doing it with Mom around, so I called him at work to see if he wanted to do lunch. I was amazed that he said "Yes" without any hesitation. He was really pretty open to the idea, suggesting the little deli right down the street from his office.

Dad was waiting when I got there. He walked over to me as I parked my car. "Good parking job. I taught you well. You'll always do all right if you just listen to your old man, Sam."

"Hi, Dad." I gave him a big hug, and we walked together into the deli. He knew the menu like the back of his hand. He probably ate here four days out of five. It took me a while to study the menu to see what I wanted. It also gave me a few seconds to get my breath and ground myself. *I can do this. Even if it blows up, it is worth a try. I can do it.*

"Sammy, are you ever going to order? As you kids say, 'Hellooo?' Get a move on; I've got to get back to work."

"Okay, okay, I'm on it." I placed my order, paid, and found a table for us. They called our number, and Dad went to get our tray. More time for me to breathe and try to decide just how I was going to approach this. It sure seemed like a good idea when I called. *How do I get myself into these messes?* Eating was enough of a diversion to buy me a few minutes.

Finally, Dad said, "What's this about, Sam? I don't think you've ever called me to do anything. Are you as upset as your mother that Brian is moving out? I think it's about time, myself. Jesus, I had three kids by the time I was his age. Your mother gets herself all upset with stuff like this. She should just let you kids be. You're all adults now. She needs to get a grip. Did you hear that…'get a grip'? Your old Dad is pretty hip, right Sam?"

"Yeah. Sure, Dad. Actually, it's not about Brian. I just wanted to talk to you, away from the house, Mom, Grandma. I never have a chance to be alone with you." I was struggling here. Dad, of course, was no help.

"Samantha, your mother told me that you're in therapy. Is that what this is about? Are you going to ask me if I'm happy? Your mother told me to tell you that I'm happy." He had a good laugh at that. "I don't know if I am or not. I just do my job and then come home and watch TV. I'm not unhappy—at least I don't think I am." He seemed kind of lost in his own reverie for a second.

I interrupted his thoughts. "Dad, you might think I'm crazy, but what I want to know is…Do you love me?" It was out. I'd said it. *Oh, my God. Breathe, Samantha!*

"Do I love you? You want to know if I love you. Of course, I love you. I love all my kids. You were all good kids. Brian was so good at football. I always felt bad that he didn't pursue a football career. He would have had to go to college though, and he didn't want to do that. You were always the one who was good at schoolwork. Brian never liked it."

"Dad, wait a minute." This exchange was clearly heading in the wrong direction. "You are going to think this is really crazy, but could you just say it again without adding anything about Brian? Please just humor me." I think I was sounding a little frantic.

"What? Your mother always said you were jealous of Brian. I never thought you were, but this is stupid. I can't talk about your brother? What is your problem, Sam? I don't think that therapy is doing you much good if I can't even talk about your brother." Dad seemed to be getting really agitated. I needed to get this over with.

"Dad, Dad, calm down. This isn't about me being jealous of Brian. It's just hard for me to hear what you said about me when you changed the subject so fast. I swear it's got nothing to do with Brian. By the way, it's perfectly normal for a child to be jealous of a younger sibling. I'm only human." I just couldn't resist adding that little tidbit. "So can you tell me again that you love me? Please?"

Dad was clearly losing his patience. "This is nuts. Yes, I love you. Now are you satisfied? I hope that was worth the price of my lunch." Dad was clearly uncomfortable and ready to move on. He had had enough of this 'feeling stuff'—that was clear.

"How are you doing with the new living arrangements? He changed the subject artfully. "Your mother tells me that you are never home. Is that because you are trying to avoid Tim and Sarah? I always liked Sarah, by the way. I always thought she was a good kid. You two seemed to really have fun together. I never did believe that she was a lesbian. Your mother and sister were all up in arms about that for a few years when you two were in high school. These crazy women—you were never like them, Sam. Well, I'm done eating, and I need to get back to work. Anything else you wanted to talk about?"

"No, Dad, at least not now. Thanks for agreeing to have lunch. I'd really like it if you didn't feel compelled to tell Mom our whole conversation. Could it just be between the two of us?" I had visions of Dad going over every detail of our conversation and Mom dissecting it like we were both frogs.

"Hell, don't you know by now, Sam? I don't tell your mother anything. I learned that a long time ago. If I tell her something, I never hear the end of it. And, I hear about it from everybody else. That is not a pleasant way to live. I just do my thing. It's your mother who can't keep her yap shut. The best advice I've got for you is, don't tell your mother anything that you don't want everyone else in the family to know. See you later, honey. Thanks for lunch."

He was gone. He just got up and walked out. I sat at the table for quite a while just replaying what had happened in my mind. *He said it! He told me that he loved me!* He didn't do it very well, or the way I had imagined he might do it, but he said it. At least he hadn't yelled like Maggie's father had done. I was glad that she told me that story though. It helped me now to sort through all that Dad had said. I was really able to hear the "I love you." I was also glad that I had asked him to repeat it. He had shifted the attention from me to all three of us and then to Brian and that didn't feel good. Hearing those words felt good. I knew that I needed to 'freeze frame' that moment, because most likely I wouldn't hear it again—unless I asked, of course. I bet my dad had never said those words to the other two kids—I wonder if he says them to Mom. Oh well, not my business.

As I got up to leave, I felt an incredible sense of happiness and peace. "Wow, my dad loves me!" I said softly to myself. Who would think that three little words could be so powerful? As I walked out the door, I noticed that there was a policeman ticketing my car. *Shit!* I was so nervous about the meeting with my dad that I'd forgotten to feed the meter. I walked up to the car as he finished writing the ticket. Instead of putting the ticket on the windshield, he handed it to me.

"I'm sorry, Miss. I didn't see you. I would have probably let it go if I'd seen you coming." He seemed so sweet.

I felt the familiar tightness in my chest. *Kindness— Wow, what an effect it has on me.* "That's okay, officer. My dad just told me that he loves me." I was grinning like an idiot. I could have cared less about a ticket. I was flying.

He laughed out loud. "Well, I'm glad to hear that, Little Missy. You have a great day."

I just couldn't resist sharing my happiness. "If you have any daughters, you might want to tell them that you love them. If you've got sons, they probably would like to hear it, too." *What was I doing, telling this poor cop how to handle his kids? I had gone off the deep end. Geez, I am making a fool of myself.*

"Don't you worry about that. My kids never go to bed without me telling them that I love them. In this business, you never know what is going to happen."

His words hit me like a ton of bricks. "Thanks for all you do. Have a good one!" I drove away, thinking of everything that had happened. *Why did I have this lingering wish that my dad had been a cop? Hey, he probably would still be unwilling to say what he was feeling. That's just my dad.*

I had a bad feeling in the pit of my stomach. "Okay, what is going on?" It seemed to help to say it out loud. "I am triggered…but why?" I heard a little voice from deep inside me say, 'I want my dad to be like him.' I felt my heart hurting. "Oh, my gosh! I hear you! You are sad because Dad can't say 'I love you' to you like that policeman says it to his kids. It's okay to be sad. It's okay to cry if you need to…I'm right here and I love you." It was amazing. I felt better immediately. And, I didn't even need to cry. *Wow!*

I don't even know how I got back to work. Good ol' Lizzie was just doing her thing. Thank God. I was in a sort of daze. So much had happened; first, hearing those words from Dad had such an impact on me. Then having the 'little voice' show up, reacting to the policeman—that was really powerful! *Maybe I need to do some anger work on why he'd never said it before. No, I really don't. I don't feel angry at him. He just couldn't do it. He still can't without being coached, but that is not about me. He was probably sober.* That was a sobering thought. *How many times have I interacted with my dad without alcohol in the picture? Not many.*

I reached for my cell phone and dialed his number. "Hey Dad, can we do lunch like once a month? I promise I won't ask so many questions. I'd just like to spend some time with you."

"Sure kid, just give me a call." Dad hung up. I sat listening to the dial tone. *Okay, I can do this!*

chapter 12

"Oh, Samantha, I'm so excited for you! How great is it that things turned out well. I'm really impressed that you were able to ask your dad to repeat himself. Even though it's hard to ask for, doesn't it make it much easier to 'let it in'? What an accomplishment for you. You have really taken the things you've learned and used them to your advantage. If you remember, I said to start small. Asking your dad to tell you he loves you is no *small* thing—it's huge. You are amazing." Maggie just sat back, looking at me.

"I do feel good. It is really nice to just sit with you and let it sink in again." Maggie created such a peaceful space that it felt good being here. "How can it be so powerful when it was really pretty lame. He didn't do it the way I wished he would at all. But he did it. I just keep going back to that."

"I know it wasn't perfect, but it was really, really, good. Your parents are both really good people who are just doing what was done to them. I'm glad that you are coming to grips with their limitations, and your own ability to take care of yourself, and get your needs met with them. Remember when I talked to you about that Regressed Child state? Well, when we are stuck in that place, we expect our parents to somehow be perfect; but at the same time we expect them to accept us the way we are. You just can't have it both ways. Either we all get to be human, or we all have to be perfect—since no one is perfect, I vote for letting us all be human." We both laughed at that.

"When the Regressed part did show up after my exchange with that cop, I handled it. I was amazed at how quickly I felt resolve. It was amazing. Maggie, I just can't believe how much I've grown since I started seeing you. I can't believe how different I am. I feel so much more in control of my emotions and therefore, my life. I really think that I've got this now."

"Oh, I almost forgot to tell you that Joann said she's recommending me for a promotion. She's been watching the way that I've been working with people, and she wants me to manage more. I'll be taking over parts of her job. I've been using what I've learned in therapy at work, and it is certainly paying off. I will get a substantial raise. I'll probably just keep the apartment after Tim and Sarah move. I'll be able to afford it now. Everything just seems to be falling into place."

Maggie looked at me and smiled. "You are simply radiant, Samantha. You look like a woman who knows herself. You are 'in your power,' as I like to say. I think that Joann sees it, as do others. People are just naturally attracted to others who exude confidence. The more you work at getting in touch with your feelings and needs and expressing them—appropriately, of course—the more people will be seeking you out. A good example is Joann. You are finally allowing people to see the real you."

"A healthy woman stands tall with her arms outstretched to the heavens." As she said the words, Maggie stretched both arms up. She looked powerful and strong. "Basically, that woman is saying, 'Here I am, world.' That is the way I see you right now. You are a strong, courageous woman. It takes real courage to tell people who you are. It takes courage because not everyone is going to like you. The old Samantha would never have been able to stand like that. The old Samantha valued other people's love and acceptance over everything—including her own feelings and needs."

"When someone said, 'I don't like this thing about you'—whatever that thing was—you changed yourself, or tried to, to please that person. If you remember that image I just modeled of the woman with her hands in the air, think about her pulling one of her hands down. Every time that you changed yourself to please someone else, you contorted yourself into something that is 'not you.' The problem is that when we do that, we end up in some sort of contorted ball; and then the person says, 'I love you.' What do we do then? If we stayed in the contorted ball, we would whither or at least feel really, really uncomfortable. If we stand up straight, reach our hands toward the heavens and proclaim, 'This is the real me,' we risk losing that person's love. It's a real dilemma. Many women fall prey to contorting themselves to keep a significant other's love. I don't just mean a partner. We do it to please parents, co-workers, and many others."

"You are a brave woman, Samantha Daley. I'm proud to know you and to be part of your process." Maggie seemed really touched by my progress.

"Thank you. I appreciate your support." I felt a little tearful as I said the words. I was pleased with myself that I was able to really hear her and not brush it off. *Wow, maybe I am making progress. I actually 'let in' the compliment.*

"Talking about being courageous," I continued. "It went well with my dad and I held my own; but I bombed again with my mother when I talked with her on the phone. I just get triggered so fast with her. I think it's because she goes into negative mode immediately. I feel bombarded by her. With Dad I can catch my breath and deal with him. I can't seem to recover long enough to really make any connection with her. Do you have any ideas that would help?" I have no clue as to how to deal with my mother.

Maggie had her hand to her chin, listening intently to what I was saying. "I hear you criticizing yourself, Samantha. I don't really think that your encounter with your mother went that badly. You really did stay 'adult' the whole time that you were on the phone with her—even though it was difficult and you had to use the tools that you have learned. You knew you had to hang up, or you would lose your boundary, and you did that. You tried to stay present with your mother. You actually did a really good job offering support and understanding. It was your mother who was not able to hear what you were saying."

Maggie continued, "Children have a fantasy about how they want their parents to be. Adults know that their parents are just people who are doing their best—even though sometimes it is a pretty lousy best. You have to grieve the loss of the mother you've always wanted, or the mother that you hoped your mother would be. She isn't going to be that person for you, Samantha. She can't be. She doesn't have the skills. She is simply mimicking what her mother did to her. It isn't that your mother doesn't love you. She does. She just doesn't love you the way that you want her to love you. That makes it your issue."

"I would bet you that she really believes that she is helping you with her criticism—because that was how she was parented." Maggie looked at me over her glasses. "Perhaps you'll have to be the one to tell her that criticism doesn't help you. Whatever you chose to do to interact with her, go slowly. You can't expect her to understand what you are doing. She will make small changes as she can. In the meantime, let that child part of you grieve the mom you didn't have."

"I'm confused." My mind was buzzing. "Grieve. That was something Sarah had to do when her parents were killed. My parents are alive and well. How could I grieve people who were still alive?"

Maggie smiled. "I know it's confusing, Samantha. Remember how we talked about all the 'parts' inside you in our second session? Those 'parts' have feelings about your mom. That Teenager had lots of angry feelings, right? Well, there are other feelings because there are also lots of fantasies about what life would have been like with your image of the perfect mom. You need to let all the parts talk to you about the mom they 'made up' to substitute for the mom who wasn't doing a very good job. That is the mom you need to grieve. To grow up means to face the reality that you are stuck with the hand you were dealt. You don't have to be happy about it, but eventually, if you want to be happy, you have to accept it—and her."

"We all do it, Samantha," Maggie continued. "None of us have a perfect life. There are always things that we wish we could change. Wishing is what children do. Adults accept what is. That doesn't mean that adults then have to settle for what is. Adults know that they have the power to change what is. That is why you came to therapy. You knew on some level that you could *do* something about your life. That is healthy. And you are doing it. A lot of people never come to that awareness. You are one of the lucky ones."

"I don't feel lucky. Why does this have to be so hard?" I think I must have looked pretty dejected.

Maggie laughed. "Samantha, I'm sorry that it's hard, but there is nothing we can do about that. You have come so far in these six sessions, it's amazing. It may be hard, but the good news is—it's not impossible. You are doing it. You came in here feeling really confused about the direction of your life. Look at you today—things are just coming together for you."

"At one point," she continued, "you made reference to a puzzle. I think you said that you felt like some of the pieces of the puzzle were starting to come together. That was an interesting metaphor because it's one that I use all the time. When people walk in that door, I see them as presenting me a 1000 piece puzzle—without the lid. There is no picture. I see it as my job to help the person put the puzzle together so they can see the picture and know themselves as they really are. The picture is whatever you want it to be. I think you have done a lot of work to create a really beautiful picture."

"Wow, how fascinating! We did work together. I used the skills you taught me, and I created the picture of my life so far. I just need to keep using the skills—even though it's hard. It's worth it. I can't believe how much better I feel. I have not thrown one of my famous tantrums since I started doing the anger work."

"Which reminds me," Maggie continued, "I always try to go over with people the goals they discussed in the first visit at the end of the six sessions. Of course, I'll remember your goals differently than you will, so feel free to throw out more if I miss some of them."

"You just mentioned your temper. It seems to me like you wanted to get your emotions under control. I think we can put a check mark by that goal. Done deal! You didn't say that swearing less was a goal, but I certainly saw it as one. I think that the swearing was related to your anger. I don't know if you've noticed, but you rarely swear anymore. I see that as a really good sign. You are a bright, articulate woman. There are many ways to make a point without having to use swear words." Maggie laughed out loud. "Of course sometimes nothing says it as well as a good swear word. I think the goal was probably that you have control over your speech and use those words when they fit."

"You were terribly upset about turning 30 and feeling like life had somehow passed you by. I think, looking at this radiant you, we can stop worrying about that. You seem to have come to grips with who you are and seem to like yourself just the way you are—a worthy goal, indeed."

"You never specifically said anything about wanting to figure out your relationships with your mom and dad, but it really did turn out to be the heart of your work. Because you are closing in on 30, you were no longer a girl but, you didn't seem to know how to move from being a girl to a woman. Well, you have done it now and done it beautifully. You present yourself so well that your boss has offered you a promotion at work. That is evidence that you are successful."

"Do you think that there were other things you came in here to do that you accomplished or that you feel are left to accomplish?" Maggie's eyes were sparkling.

"Actually, I think you summed it up perfectly." I was surprised that she had that kind of understanding of where I had been and where I was now. "Do you think I should be coming back?" Even though I was pretty sure I wasn't going to return, I think I wanted the validation that she didn't think that I needed to.

Maggie just smiled. "I trust you, Samantha Daley, to know what is right for you. I know that if you need more help or support, you'll call. You know I'm just a resource for you. You are making excellent decisions for yourself right now and using the tools you have learned. You are truly an amazing woman."

"In the beginning, I warned you that people may not like what you are doing. You have had some negative feedback from your mom and sister about how therapy has affected your life with them. You have also had the positive feedback from your boss, which resulted in a promotion. Therapy is a funny thing. It's something like throwing a rock in a pool of water. There are always ripples. Some of the ripples are good, some bad. You just never know how or where your changes will affect others. Now you are able to handle whatever comes up—good or bad. That's the difference between when you walked in and now."

"The only circumstance under which you might want to call me is if you find yourself in a relationship. It is hard to stay boundaried in a relationship, but it's not impossible. I often tell clients to come back and see me when they find a man. For some reason women tend to give up themselves to be with a man. You don't have to do that to be in a good relationship. In fact, if you go back to old habits—giving yourself away to please him, it probably isn't a good relationship. Two strong people can come together and be happy if they are just willing to use the skills—know yourself, listen to the other, and negotiate. It's premature to talk about this now, Samantha. I just want you to keep it in mind as another goal—down the road."

"Well, I can tell you that I'm not ready to be in a relationship just yet. I feel like I'm on a quest to know myself. I don't want to muddy the waters right now by adding someone else into the equation. I feel good about pulling myself out of the hole I was digging when I was always trying to please my family. I don't want to fall back into that hole again. When you are in a relationship, you have to take the other person's feelings into consideration. I'm afraid I'll just give in, the way I did with my parents and other boyfriends. I will never let that happen again. I've worked too hard to get this far. I won't go back." I could tell by how determined I sounded that it was really important to me.

"Wow!" Maggie exclaimed. "I really like the power I am hearing in your voice. Great!"

"Keeping the 'new me' is definitely a goal. I will never be in a relationship if it resembles what my parents have.

That might be why I'm still single. Of course, Sarah says all the men I choose are just like my dad. They aren't really present. Maybe she's right. I have heard her say it, but I never really understood what she meant until I started this process."

"I think I'm ready, Maggie, to do life on my own—at least for now. I know I can come back if I need to, and I will. I can't thank you enough for all that I've learned. I really do feel like I'm a different person. Even if the puzzle I brought in here had a picture on the top, that picture just wouldn't work for the new, improved, Samantha. I am a new woman—emphasis on the word *woman*."

Maggie and I just looked at each other for a second or two. I'm sure there were equal amounts of love and appreciation on both of our faces. Our time together was over, for now.

We both stood simultaneously. "Maggie, do you ever give a hug goodbye? If you do, I'd like one." I felt a bit like a kid asking, but I knew it was what I wanted.

"Of course, I do. I'm so impressed with your request. You sound like a woman who knows what she wants and is willing to ask for it."

"Thank you. That means a lot to me, coming from you."

We hugged. I felt tears stinging my eyes. I felt like I owed this woman my life. I know she would have argued with me. How many times had she told me that I was the one who did all the work—she just taught me the skills. I managed to say, "I appreciate all you have done for me, Maggie."

As we parted, Maggie said, "Thank you, Samantha. You come see me any time. I'm always here for you."
I believed her.

chapter 13

Wow! Time really does fly, whether you are having fun or not. I couldn't believe I was standing here waving goodbye to Sarah and Tim. The moving van had just left. Tim and Sarah were in her car on their way to their new house. A house, I can't believe they had actually decided to take the plunge and buy a house together. Spending six months with the two of them, it was clear to me that they were made for each other. Just because I was happy for them didn't mean the tears weren't flowing like a waterfall. This was going to be really, really hard.

I walked back into the house with Shiloh on my heels. She kept turning to look down the road. "They aren't coming back, baby girl. We'll go visit them, and they will visit us, but they won't be back to live with us ever again." As I said the words, I cried again. *I thought I could do this, but can I? I know I can manage the financial end, but I've never been alone in my life. This is going to be hell for a while. I'm so glad we decided that I would get full custody of you, girl.*

The apartment looked so empty when I walked in. Sarah had taken her half of everything. Now I understood how some of the women in our office felt after their divorces were final. The rooms felt so empty. We'd done some shopping so each of us had 'filled in the blanks' in the kitchen. I wasn't going to have a breakdown when I discovered the popcorn popper was gone or anything—we'd taken care of that. It was the emptiness of the rooms. Sarah's room was completely empty. I just sat in the middle of her room on the cold floor and cried some more.

"I think this is good. I'm feeling my feelings. That's what Maggie would tell me to do." My voice echoed in the empty room. "Yuck, this feels terrible. I need to get out of this room." I got up and headed for the couch. I was pretty sure we had TIVOed *Survivor*. That should keep me occupied for a while. Popcorn would also help.

On the way to the kitchen, the phone rang. "Hi, Lon," I said as I picked up the phone. I learned the hard way to look at caller ID. Caller ID also serves as an excellent boundary. If I don't want to talk to someone, I simply don't answer. It feels so good to be in control of who gets into my house, even through the phone.

"What's up, Doll? Do you want me to come over and keep you company tonight? Isn't this the big move out day?" I thought I could hear him panting on the other end of the line.

"Yes, it's move out day." I answered, "And 'No' I don't want any company tonight. It feels terrible, but in a good way. You'd never understand. I just want to be alone tonight."

"Are you crazy, Samantha? You are just going to depress yourself sitting there all by yourself. I'll get a pizza and bring it over. We can watch a little TV and see what 'comes up.'" He was laughing hysterically at his own stupid joke.

"Lon, I said, 'No.' I mean, 'No.' And don't just show up like you did the time Tim and Sarah went out of town for the weekend. There will be no repeats of that weekend. In fact, I'm still angry at you about that."

"Oh my God, get over it will you Sammy. I just wanted to have a little fun. You used to be fun, but no more. I'll give you a call some other time." The next thing I heard was a dial tone. He had hung up.

I sat there and stared at the phone in my hand. It was becoming very clear that Lon was not the person with whom I wanted to explore a healthy relationship. *Nope! No way!*

"Well, that was a real morale booster, girl." Shiloh wouldn't get two feet from me. I think she was having some kind of abandonment issues because Sarah was gone—along with some of her favorite pieces of furniture. "Let's go look in the couch and see if we can find you anything." I'd taken to hiding her bones in the couch so that she always came up with a goody when she went digging. Sure enough, she found it immediately and settled down to her chewing.

"What do I want to do right now?" I figured talking to myself was going to be something that I did a lot—I could always claim that I was talking to Shiloh. What do they say about talking to yourself—it's okay as long as you don't answer. Well, we'd just have to see how crazy I'd get being in the house all by myself.

I continued to the kitchen to get my popcorn. It just didn't seem as much fun without Sarah to make the butter. *Shit! This was not going to be easy. What about journaling? Now would be the perfect time to get out my journal and try to process what is going on.*

I wrote for some time. I did a little anger work and cried a lot. At the end of it, I felt much better. I was amazed when I looked at the clock. I had managed to survive the evening without Sarah. I had spent the first evening in my own apartment and lived to tell about it. I actually felt better. I'd been able to do a lot of the feeling work that I knew I needed to do to begin to accept the changes in my life.

I looked down to see Shiloh lying at my feet. "What is it, girl? Do you need to go out? Okay, I'm on it. Let me get my jacket." We were out the door as fast as Shiloh could drag me. It was a beautiful night. I breathed deeply. "I'm going to be fine," I said to no one at all and to everyone in the world.

When I walked in the office the next day, Janet and Joann were at my desk almost before I was. "Are you okay?" They both spoke in unison.

"Even I'm amazed, but I'm doing fine. I know I'll have some hard times. But for right now, I'm processing the feelings as I go; and I'm doing really well. Shiloh is a little more of a burden than she seemed before. Sarah and I always took turns taking her out, feeding her and stuff like that, but I'm just going to have to get used to it. I just have a lot of things that are going to change. I can handle it, but thanks so much for asking."

They walked away, somewhat dejected I think. This office was a female crisis center. One of us was always in some kind of crisis or another. I think it was a big disappointment that I wasn't turning this into a crisis. *Hey, can I help it that I'm handling it?*

The phone on my desk rang, breaking my reverie. "Hey, kiddo, are we doing lunch today?"

"Hi, Dad. Is it the first Monday already? Of course I'll meet you at the deli same time."

"See you then, honey."

"Bye, Dad." Some things never change. My dad was never going to be a man of many words. It was really unusual for him to call me though. Usually I was the one calling him to drag him to our lunch date. It had worked out kind of cool. He and I had been having lunch the first Monday of every month since our first meeting. This call tells me he might like the idea of our lunches as much as I do.

I didn't really feel the need to ask him questions any more, like the first time we went out. The funny thing is that he seems to have gotten turned on to telling me stories about his family, his youth. It's sort of like he's been waiting for someone to ask him out for lunch his whole life. I was just glad that I was the one who thought of it. We'd actually gotten closer. I was beginning to feel like I had a relationship with him.

I'd have to say that it's not exactly the kind of relationship I'd envision in a perfect world. It's sort of a one-way relationship. He doesn't ask about me or what I am doing, but if I want him to know something, I tell him, so that works. He just opened up, never with any feelings or anything like that, but with stories. He likes to tell me stories. And I love hearing them.

I finally found out why we don't see his mom and dad much. They are very strong Catholics. They could never forgive him for getting my mom pregnant, even though the marriage had lasted. Mom and Dad have been together for over 30 years. *It's amazing to me how people can do stuff like that, but hey, I was raised in a different generation.* Dad didn't seem upset when he told me, just said it in a matter-of-fact way. He did acknowledge that he'd like to see them more often because they are getting older and probably wouldn't be around much longer. I encouraged him to try to contact them. He never responded and has never said a word since. That's my dad.

The morning flew by. I was running late, and Dad was pacing in front of the deli as I parked the car. "Where the hell have you been? I've used up 15 minutes of my lunch hour waiting for you." Pleasant beginnings were not my dad's forte.

"Dad, you're twinkling! Don't try to convince me you're mad when your eyes are twinkling like that. You're an old phoney." It was funny how his gruffness didn't trigger me at all anymore. I felt like I could kid with him, like we were friends.

"I was teasing you, 'Darlin.' I just got here a couple of minutes ago myself. I got a phone call from a friend and couldn't break free."

Shocker, my dad had a friend! He did lots of stuff at church, but I don't think I'd ever seen him one-on-one with a friend. *Hmmm.* I was learning fast not to assume I knew my dad. He was way more complex than I had ever imagined him to be.

"Well, come on, let's get our order in." By this time I had the menu memorized, and more to the point, the owners had our orders memorized. We walked in and said, "We'll have our usual." It was Dad's turn to pay, so I found a table.

"I'm glad you called this morning, Dad. With Sarah moving out, it has been so hectic. I'm sure I would have forgotten."

"Are you going to be okay? With Brian gone, you could move home with your mom and me if you wanted to."

I looked at him to see if he was serious. I could see the twinkle in his eyes. "You really do know how to get to me, don't you? Mom and I would kill each other, and you know it. What a putz you are. Anyway I'm doing fine. It was hard when she left, and I'm sure I'll have more hard times until I really adjust to being alone. For now, I'm taking it one day at a time. I'll be fine, Dad. This helps a lot you know, to know that we can connect once a month like this. I really appreciate you taking the time to do this. Thanks, Dad." I was starting to tear up so I blinked a few times. I didn't want to send Dad over the edge. Tears weren't his thing.

"It's okay to cry, Samantha." Even Dad had started to use my given name. I liked it. He put his hand on my arm as he continued. "I'm not going to run screaming into the night because of a few tears. I'm glad having lunch helps you. It helps me, too."

"Samantha, remember the first time we did this? You were as jumpy as a cat on a hot tin roof. I feel the same way today. I've got something to say, and I just want you to listen. Your mother told me what your therapist said—well, she screamed it at me one night when I'd had a little too much to drink. She said that your therapist thought I was an alcoholic. It hit me hard. Your mother has been bitching about my drinking ever since we met, but I just tune her out. However, it really hit me when she said that a therapist had said that."

"A friend of mine, here at work, has been talking about attending AA meetings for years. He's a really good guy and someone I respect. I talked with him, and I've been going to AA meetings with him for the past month. I get my 30-day chip tonight, Samantha, and I'd like you to be there. Can you come?"

I couldn't move. I just sat there looking at my dad. I could feel the tears stinging my eyes but really didn't care. "I wouldn't miss it for the world. Tell me where and when. Oh my God, Dad! I am so proud of you. Why haven't you said anything? Does Mom know?"

"I'm sure she knows something's going on, but 'No' I haven't actually said anything to her. I didn't want to tell anyone because I was afraid I couldn't do it. They tell me the first 90 days are the hardest, so I hope I'm not setting both of us up for a big disappointment. I just wanted someone to be there to see me get my chip." My dad looked like a little boy who needed very much to be told he'd done a good job.

"Are you telling me that no one knows but me?" I was incredulous.

"Nope, nobody else knows. And, you better keep it that way. I don't want you blabbing this to anybody. This is our secret—until I'm ready to share it. I thought I could trust you. I can, can't I?"

"Of course, Dad, I won't tell a soul." I saw my father differently in that moment. I felt a kind of respect I had never felt. He'd always seemed like such a wimp, putting up with my mother's criticism with no retort. I liked the man I was looking at. Wow!

Dad gave me all the details, and we exchanged a quick hug after lunch. On the way back to the office I couldn't help but think of Maggie DeWitt. I wondered if on some cosmic level she knew that she had influenced not only my life but the lives of others around me.

Then I remembered what she had said that last day. Something about my changing being like a stone tossed in a pond—it creates ripples. I think was I experiencing one of those ripples watching my dad and all the changes he was going through. He'd also mentioned at lunch that he had written a long letter to his parents—another ripple. He said it had something to do with his AA program. He's still waiting for a reply. Here was a chance for these old people to reconcile with their son. Would they take the opportunity?

This all seemed so miraculous to me. What did Maggie say?—"There is magic in this work." Now I believed her. The whole world seemed to have a special glow today. It's not like everything is perfect—it isn't. I am still a long way from having any kind of relationship with my mom or sister. I do get along really well with Amanda, Brian's girlfriend. She's confided to me that she is pregnant. Oh boy, I can't wait to see what happens when this bomb goes off. This will really send Mom over the edge, but hey—she'll survive. She'll call in 'crisis mode,' and then she'll calm down. Some things never change.

No, things aren't perfect. I guess nothing ever is. The one perfect thing is me and my process. I've learned how to check in with myself and to know myself. Maggie always asked, "Are you feeling happy, sad, angry, or scared?" The answer always used to be sad, angry or scared. Today my answer is, "I'm feeling really, really happy!"

What About Me?

A Novel Approach to Personal Growth

APPENDICES I, II, III, IV, V

Copyright 2009

Jacqueline M. Dierks, Ph.D.

ALL RIGHTS RESERVED

appendix I

Healthy Adult Interaction

1. I know what I FEEL. (Happy, Sad, Angry, Scared)
2. I can EXPRESS that feeling appropriately.
3. I know what I NEED.
4. I can EXPRESS that need appropriately.

These four steps cover the "I" part of the adult experience—knowing yourself well enough to represent yourself in a relationship.

5. I can LISTEN to others' feelings/needs.
6. I can VALIDATE his/her feelings and needs as equal to my own feelings and needs.

This is the "other" part of the adult experience—you put your needs on hold long enough to really hear the other person's feelings and needs.

7. I can NEGOTIATE so that both of us get our needs met.

This is the "us" aspect of the adult experience—a place where both parties feel heard, validated, and loved.

appendix II

Passive/Aggressive Behavior

WE ARE ALL passive-aggressive sometimes. We are conditioned in this culture not to be direct and not to ask for what we need. When we do ask for what we need directly, we are deemed "selfish." When we use indirect means to gain an end, we are being passive-aggressive. However, there is a continuum of behavior on the passive-aggressive scale. We need to be aware when other people are extremely passive-aggressive because it is very difficult to be in relationships with these people—no matter what type of relationship it is, family-of-origin, significant other, workplace, social situations. Hopefully, this handout will help you to identify passive-aggressive people more readily and give you some tips for dealing with them. If you are a passive-aggressive person, it may help you to be aware of your behavior and change it.

A TEST FOR PASSIVE/AGGRESSIVE BEHAVIOR

O=Often   S=Sometimes   R=Rarely   N=Never

1. Use of sarcasm   O S R N

2. Ask a lot of questions   O S R N

3. Take responsibility   O S R N

4. Able to say, "I'm wrong."   O S R N

5. Keep promises   O S R N

6. Make excuses   O S R N

7. Feel misunderstood   O S R N

8. Blame others   O S R N

9. Talk behind other's back   O S R N

10. Procrastinate   O S R N

Scoring: Give 0 points for each Never, 1 for Sometimes, 2 for Rarely, 3 for Often.

EXCEPT FOR 3, 4, 5—In these three items you **reverse score**, give 3 points for Never, 2 points for Sometimes, 1 point for Rarely, and 0 for Often.

Total score:
If your score is:

0-9 = You are pretty normal.

10-20 = You have passive/aggressive tendencies.

20-30 = You might want to talk to a professional to help you get your needs met.

This is a gross estimate. Please don't consider this a definitive answer about yourself or anyone else—it is a rough estimate of passive-aggressive tendencies. If you take the test and get a high score, all is not lost. Read the rest of the handout and see if you can be more direct in getting your needs met. If someone you love gets a high score on this measure, make sure that your boundaries are well intact when dealing with this person. S/He probably has a way of "getting to you."

DISCUSSION OF TEST ITEMS

1. **Use of sarcasm**: Passive-Aggressive people use sarcasm to mask their anger. This also includes "jokes" that aren't funny—they are at your expense; veiled criticism that can be taken a couple of different ways; "benign" observations, sometimes called "constructive criticism." There is also a possibility that the person will use "unspoken" sarcasm, e.g., buy you an item of clothing labeled Small when you wear Large; buy things that you don't like or that you're allergic

to; invite people you don't like to functions they have planned for you; and/or do things that you have stated you don't want done. This type of behavior is hard to define and difficult to confront because it is so elusive. These people seem to be masters of the "dig."

2. **Ask a lot of questions**: Passive-aggressive people "check out" the other person by asking a lot of questions rather than stating their need directly.

3. **Take responsibility**: The passive-aggressive person has a talent for making things "about you." It is very difficult for this person to take personal responsibility in any area of life. If you are unhappy with them, for any reason, they find a way to make it not their fault. For example, if you are unhappy that they are late for an appointment, it gets turned around in such a way that you feel wrong for expecting him/her to be on time. S/He may say things like, "And you are NEVER late? You are too sensitive. You are obsessive."

4. **Able to say, "I'm wrong."**: The passive-aggressive person cannot be wrong. It is as if it somehow erodes their whole being to make one mistake. If confronted, they will argue a point until it is ridiculous, and on some level both of you know it—but s/he will not give in.

5. **Keep promises**: This is a little more abstract than the simple phrase seems. It means that the person cannot be trusted to do things they say they will do. For

example, if s/he says, "I know you are in a hurry today and need your suit from the cleaners. Don't worry, I'll pick it up." What they have promised may not happen because passive-aggressive people have a way of "forgetting" or "time just gets away"—they punish people by not doing things they have said that they will do.

6. **Make excuses**: The passive/aggressive person always has an excuse why s/he didn't do what was expected. One way of making excuses is to tell a lie. Lying is always passive-aggressive—even white lies. Lying is a way of avoiding conflict.

7. **Feel misunderstood**: Because people have reactions to the passive/aggressive person and his/her lack of responsibility, s/he often tells the world how misunderstood or unappreciated they are. They are unable to see their part in why the world does not understand or appreciate them. S/He is the victim of an uncaring world.

8. **Blame others**: The passive-aggressive person must blame someone for his/her unhappiness, and everyone else is the target of their blame. "If only you were different, my life would be fine," that is the theme song of the passive-aggressive person. They, of course, are not willing to discuss with the other person what s/he is doing that makes them so miserable.

9. **Talk behind other's back**: The passive-aggressive person always has a lot to say about other people and how they should live their lives, but never to the person's face. You may hear all about your failures or your successes from relatives, friends, co-workers, but you will never hear it directly from a passive-aggressive person.

10. **Procrastination**: This *can be* passive-aggressive behavior. Many people just have procrastination as a part of their character. It is hard to determine whether someone who has made a commitment to do something and then isn't doing it is being passive-aggressive.

HOW DO I RECOGNIZE IT?—LOOK INWARD, AT YOUR FEELINGS!

You feel confused... The passive-aggressive person makes promises and doesn't follow through. If you ask about it, you are made to feel "wrong" for asking. The passive-aggressive person is good at telling "funny" jokes that don't feel funny to you, in fact you often feel attacked. If you try to confront the behavior, it is turned back on you. You are made to feel like you are the problem because you can't take a joke. The hallmark of the passive-aggressive person is the double message—a verbal message and a feeling message. The verbal message can be sweet or seem benign; the feeling message behind it is angry or hostile—like a snowball with a rock in it. S/He tries to look like the "nice guy/good person/martyr" but can't pull it off because s/he is so angry and, that anger is always leaking. You end up feeling confused because you are hearing one thing but feeling something different. When the two are in conflict, the words and the deeds, it's crazy-making. Always trust what people do, they can *say* anything.

You feel wrong... You start out with a simple situation. Perhaps you are upset because the other person is late—you end up feeling like you were wrong for bringing up the subject. The passive-aggressive person blames others for everything. If s/he is late, it is because of someone else. Therefore, you have no right to be angry with him/her. Somehow things seem to boomerang—you believe that you have a legitimate complaint, and it ends up getting turned against you. You get the feeling that you can't win.

You feel betrayed... Passive-aggressive people will tell you one thing to your face, and you will hear that they have told someone else the exact opposite. They talk behind your back—and everyone else's. They do not have the courage to be honest. These are not trustworthy people when their needs conflict with others.

You feel "less-than"... You can never meet the needs of passive-aggressive people, because they will never tell you exactly what they need. Therefore, you always end up feeling "less-than." It is important to realize that you are an okay person. It is not your problem that they cannot be clear with you about what they need. It is also important to realize that they will probably never be clear; therefore, you will never feel successful with this person nor will anyone else.

You feel responsible... The passive-aggressive person is unable to take responsibility for his or her own life. Everyone else gets blamed for his or her unhappiness. The problem is that nothing anyone does makes him/her happy. Always remember—they have to know what will make them happy and tell you. You cannot read minds, nor can you fix their unhappiness.

You hear lots of questions...(More about this later.) For now just understand that most questions are passive-aggressive. Behind every question is a feeling and a need. If you feel uncomfortable with a question from someone, ask the person if they can state the feeling and need behind their question.

HOW DO I DEAL WITH IT?—VERY CAREFULLY!!!

It is important to remember that the direct approach that we work on in therapy is not necessarily going to work with this type of person. S/He is not in touch with the anger that s/he leaks. That does not mean you shouldn't try to be direct. I encourage you to start with something small that does not have a lot of meaning for you. If the person responds well to your first attempt, then go on to something more important. Keep in mind that you are the one who is the healthiest. If you begin to lose your boundaries, STOP. You only set yourself up for pain if you know you are not okay and you keep trying to interact.

Here are some things you can try:

a) I imagine you are angry with me. Just tell me what the problem is.
b) It's okay to be angry with me.
c) When you say, "Call when you aren't too busy," I imagine that you are angry that I don't call you more often. It's okay to tell me what's on your mind.
d) I imagine that you are blaming me because you did not get what you wanted. Is that true?
e) What you want is important to me. If you'll tell me what you want from me, I'll try to do it.

If you try these things and you get denial, anger, blame, accusations, and/or silence, then I suggest that you use that response as information and accept that you may not have a really deep, meaningful relationship with this person. That does not mean that you let the "Rebellious Teenager" put up a barrier; it simply means that you strengthen the boundary and support yourself—getting support from other places if you need it when you have to deal with this person.

I don't suggest sharing a lot of feelings with the passive-aggressive person. A passive-aggressive person may use your feelings against you. You must first and foremost take care of yourself. That means that you do not open yourself to an attack from this person. You make clear, "I need," statements without going into your feelings, especially if they are vulnerable feelings.

It is also important that you work on letting go of the fantasy relationship that the feeling part of you wants and believes can exist. You have to grieve the loss of the relationship the way you would grieve if you literally lost someone through death. If you can grieve the fantasy relationship, it will allow you to accept the person as they are and have some kind of minimal relationship based on his/her abilities. In other words, you will be able to see his/her meager attempts at "loving you" as the best s/he can do. You will be able to be at peace even though they s/he never be.

MORE ABOUT QUESTIONS—SOME ANSWERS!

Passive-aggressive people are really angry people who have no way of expressing their anger. They are usually passive-aggressive because a) they learned it from a passive/aggressive parent; or, b) they had an aggressive parent with whom they could not share feelings. Consequently, they cannot be direct about much of anything, especially anger. They learned to use indirect techniques to feel some power—they controlled or manipulated a situation to get their needs met. For example, Johnny wants to go to the show tonight. His mother comes home from work, and he asks, "How was work?" He is taking mom's emotional temperature. He will know from her response whether to continue; and if he's going to continue, what line to take. He will probably continue to ask questions like, "Are you going out tonight?" When he has tested the water to his satisfaction, he will either ask directly to go to the show or give a story about "his friends are going." If she is really upset, he may just say nothing and sneak out his bedroom window.

Remember, all he wants is to go to the show—*that* is the one question that may not ever be asked, but he will ask a thousand others to try to gain a successful outcome—getting to the show.

If you feel irritated by questions, it is probably because you imagine the other person is trying to control or manipulate you. This may or may not be true. All you can do is check it out with the person. A simple way to do that is to say, "I feel uncomfortable with your questions. I am imagining that you have something else you want or need from me. I need you to tell me about that." For example, a husband who has been up for a while comes into the bedroom where his wife is just waking up and asks, "Are you getting up?" She responds, "I don't know." He asks again, "Are you coming to the kitchen?" She responds again, "I don't know." Most likely, the unstated need here is—I'm up, I'm lonely, I'd like you to come to the kitchen and eat while I do. If the husband could just say those words, the wife knows what he wants and can decide if she wants to meet his need.

Many times passive-aggressive people feel victimized by their environment. No one takes care of them the way that they want to be taken care of. One way to recognize passive-aggressive behavior is to hear the victim/martyr language of "You always or You never." Because it is so difficult for passive-aggressive people to take responsibility for themselves, they say little about what they want but then blame the significant other for their unhappiness. For example, "You never take me anywhere." "You never touch me." "You always are out with your friends while I stay home and do nothing." The part left unsaid is that the person has never a) asked for what s/he needed, or b) confronted the inappropriate behavior of the significant other in a healthy way.

Examples of Passive/Aggressive Behavior

1) A mother continually tells a child that she doesn't look good in a certain color and then buys her things that color and, of course, is angry if she doesn't wear them.

2) A mother shames her child for not having any friends, but when the child tries to bring friends home, the mother rages at the child for not caring about her—because having friends over will mess up the house.

3) A woman gets yelled at for not carrying money with her when her husband needs some cash for a show. The next time she carries cash, and he belittles her for trying to be "Mrs. Big Bucks."

4) A father encourages his son to talk to him but then belittles the child by saying, "That's a stupid thing to be scared about."

5) Comparing yourself to someone else, putting yourself in a positive light: For example, "I make way less money that you do, and yet I don't have any money problems."

6) Any guilt trip is passive-aggressive. For example, "Go ahead, go play cards with your friends. I'll be fine by myself all night."

7) Attributing something to someone else is passive-aggressive. For example, "My mom was really angry that you didn't call me when you said you would."

9) Chronic lateness can be passive-aggressive.

10) Lying is passive-aggressive. This is one habit that is worth breaking. You will like yourself much better.

11) Hiding things from others is passive-aggressive. For example, a woman buys a new dress that costs more than she thinks it should. She hangs it in the back of the closet so that her husband won't see it.

12) You "do" things for others and then feel angry because they do not appreciate it. Examine your motives. Is there an unstated "string" attached? If there is, then tell the person up front what the "string" is. For example, "I really went out of my way to get this for you. I need to know that you appreciate it."

13) Doing things for other people that are right for you but not for them. For example, a mother-in-law comes to visit her son and daughter-in-law and proceeds to clean and rearrange their kitchen cupboards—her way.

appendix III

A Format for Journaling

My clients report to me that they learn faster if they journal about stressful experiences. First, purchase a notebook. A spiral notebook will work fine, but if you want it to be special, then get a really nice book. You might also purchase a tiny notebook to fit in a pocket or purse so that you can do "in the moment" processing. When you experience yourself being "triggered," try to write down what happened. You can either do all the writing in the moment or if you don't have time, do the "processing" later.

A: Triggering event: (Just leave this blank at first if you can't figure out the source of the trigger.)

B: Feelings: (Stick with basic feelings like happy, sad, angry or scared.)

C: Critic: (Write out all the "You statements" you hear in your head directed at yourself.)

D: Teenager: (Write out all the "You statements" you hear in your head directed at other people. Have you said them out loud or are they just in your head?)

After you have listened to all the "parts," sit back in your chair and take a few deep breaths. When you're grounded, go to the adult state.

E: Adult: What would a healthy adult say to the feeling part?...to the critic?...to the teenager? What would a healthy adult say to the other person after the triggering episode?

REMEMBER:

1) Start with the loudest voice you hear if you are hearing a lot of self-talk. If you are not experiencing self-talk, start with the feelings.

2) You probably will not hear all the voices during a triggering event. Just write what you hear. The voices fall into categories by the language they use, i.e., self-blame—Critic; attacking others—FU teen; helplessness—regressed part.

3) You may not know what the triggering event was until you have done the writing from the regressed and reactive places. Keep writing, letting the feelings out while you are writing.

Examples of Journaling

Example Number 1

A woman was out shopping, and when she got home, she realized that she was not okay. Something had triggered her while she was out. She got out her journal and began to write.

A: Triggering event: *I have no idea what triggered me.*

B: Regressed feeling part: *I'm feeling…sad. I feel sad. I don't know why I'm feeling sad but, I feel like crying. I am crying. I am so sad.*

As she cried, she "saw" (became conscious of) the front door of the Target store she'd been shopping at. On the door was an advertisement for Father's Day. Her dad had died in December, and the advertisement triggered the sad feelings about losing him. She hadn't even consciously seen the advertisement. The sign on the door was the "triggering event."

She let herself cry about her father's death. She was sad because this was her first Father's Day without a dad. After she cried she felt much better.

C: Critic:

D: Teenager:

E: Adult: *It's okay to cry. It's sad to not have a dad on Father's Day. Dad, I miss you. It's hard to see advertisements about Father's Day knowing that I don't have you to call or celebrate with. I love you.*

As you can see by this example, you will not always hear all the voices. Start with the feelings when you aren't sure what is happening. The feelings will lead you to the "triggering event."

Example Number 2

In this case it is clear what the "triggering event" is. What is important is to get at what is really going on. Why is the person triggered and feeling so shamed? As the journaling progresses, it's clear that the writer has projected her critical father onto everyone in the meeting. She has regressed and is feeling the same kinds of shame she felt as a child when Dad was critical. In her adult, she is able to confront the critic and Dad and stop critical self-talk. The key in this example is that the person started journaling with the CRITIC. Only after hearing what the Critic had to say, could she get in touch with the origins of the problem and then get in touch with all her feelings.

A: Triggering event: *I was at a meeting. There were lots of people present at the meeting. Part of the meeting consisted of a question and answer session. I asked a question of the president of the company that he could not answer. I felt like a complete idiot—I was triggered. On the way home, I was telling myself how stupid I was for asking that question.*

C: Critic. *You are so stupid. I can't believe that you would ask THAT question. That wasn't even the subject that he was talking about. You looked like an idiot. Everyone in that room thinks that you are stupid. Who do you think you are, jumping up like that to ask a question?*

B: Feelings (Regressed part): *I'm scared, and I'm sad. I'm scared people will think I'm dumb. I want people to like me.*

I want people to think I'm smart. Nobody's going to like me. When I think no one will like me, then I feel sad.

Allow the feelings to come out. If you are feeling tearful, it's okay to cry.

E: Adult: *to the Regressed part—You didn't do anything wrong. You have a right to ask a question. I love you, and you aren't stupid.*

Adult: *to the Critic—You aren't helping. It's unfortunate that my boss didn't know the answer to that question but I'm not wrong or bad for asking it. Other people are not critical like you. Stop criticizing me. You sound just like Dad. Well, I'm not little and you aren't my dad. Whenever I hear, "Who do you think you are?" I know that you are still living in my head, Dad, and I'm angry about that. Stop it! Stop criticizing me!*

You may need to do anger work at Dad to get the Critic to be quiet. If so, do the anger work and then return to the Critic.

Example Number 3

In this example all the 'parts' have a voice. You cannot confront a person, in this case the boss, without first grounding yourself. If you try before you are prepared, you will revert to one of the parts and it won't go well. We've all started out trying to confront someone and ended up in tears (regressed, feeling part) or gotten angry and just walked out (silent FU part). Using this method, you ground yourself and don't "lose it."

A: Triggering event: *My boss yelled at me. He said, "You should have known better than to do that."*

B: Regressed feeling part: *I'm feeling scared. I feel little. I don't know what to do. I don't want to go back to work. He scares me. He's mean to me.*

C: Critic: *You deserved to be yelled at. Look at the lousy job you did. He's right. You don't know anything.*

D: Silent Rebellious Teenager: *I'm pissed! How dare he talk to me that way! Fuck him! I am quitting this stupid job. I can get a job any place. I don't need this shit. I am angry. I want him to know I'm angry. He has no right to talk to me like that.*

E: Adult: *I'm breathing. I'm okay now.*

…to the Regressed part: *I'm right here. The boss was frustrated. It's okay to cry. I'll listen to you. I'll talk to him. He's not Dad. I know Dad said those same words to you all the time. I'm not little anymore. I'm an adult and, I can take care of myself with the boss.*

　…to the Critic: *Okay, that's enough! I made a mistake. Stop it! I don't need to hear any more about how stupid I am.*

　…to the Silent Rebellious Teenager: *You have a right to be angry. He was inappropriate. I'll tell him tomorrow that I acknowledge that I made a mistake, but I do not want to be addressed in that manner again.*

appendix IV

Formula for Healthy Confrontation

When someone does or says something that is upsetting to you, a healthy way to confront that behavior is to use this formula.

When you say or do _____,

   Be specific. Examples: When you don't call when you are running late; or when you raise your voice; or when you forget to do something you have said you will do.

   Do not use generalities. Examples: When you don't respect me; or when you don't care about me.

I feel _____. (Happy, sad, angry, scared)

Do not follow the word "feel" with the word "that". If you do, you are talking about beliefs or thoughts. Examples: I feel that you don't care about me. That is a "you statement" dressed up to look like an "I statement." Only use feeling words after the word "feel."

Because I imagine _____.

This is the "meat" of the exchange. You are causing your own discomfort because of your fantasies associated with the exchange. You need to get real and tell the person what you are telling yourself about what happened. For example, "When you forget to call me after you've said that you will, I feel angry because I imagine that I am not important to you." You are upsetting yourself by telling yourself you are not important. You are imposing your fantasy on to the other person. The only way you can know what is going on with another person is to ask. So "check out" your fantasy by asking the person if that is true for them. You have to be willing to give up your fantasy if the person denies that it is their reality.

If the person says, "You are important to me. I was caught in traffic with a dead cell phone and no charger." You have to be able to breathe and "let go" of your fantasy. Sometimes it's pretty hard to do that. You may have to ask the person to repeat that a few times.

Sharing your thoughts and insecurities is only appropriate when you are dealing with people who are "intimates." It is probably not appropriate in the office, or if you are dealing with people who might throw those insecurities back at you at a later time.

What I need from you now is _____.

Usually we need an apology from someone who has hurt us. Since each event is unique, only you will know for sure what it is that you need. Take some time to look inside, and then ask for what you need to be finished with this. If you hold a grudge and can't let something go, it hurts you as much as it does the other person.

What I need from you in the future is _____.

In the case of this example, the person may need the other person to pull over into a gas station and make the phone call in the future. If it is the case that the person is driving alone, late at night, the partner may worry. Again, only the individual knows what s/he needs.

appendix V

Anger Work

THE CLEAREST INDICATOR that you need to do anger work is when you are over-reacting to someone or something. When we over-react, we have been triggered by something. No matter what feeling you are experiencing, (happiness, sadness, anger, or fear) if the feeling is over-whelming, you have been triggered. If you are angry, try doing the anger work as suggested here. Remember, yelling at another person is NEVER appropriate. This work is to be done in the privacy of your home or car—anywhere that you are away from people. When you have done the work and regained control of your emotions, THEN you return to the person with whom you are having the disagreement to negotiate. This is a great exercise to do when you have called a "time out."

Steps in Doing Anger Work

1. Someone (Person A) says or does something and, you feel "too much" energy—you are over-reacting. This "intensity of energy" is information that tells you that you are *"projecting"* someone else (Person B) onto this person.

2. Begin your anger work at Person A. Make all the "you statements" you can think of pertaining to the situation. Try to make general statements. Use a tape recorder if you want so that you can play back the "you statements."

3. Ask yourself "Who else could I say these words to? When have I felt like this before?" You are trying to identify who deserves the bulk of the anger you are feeling. Pay attention to any pictures or past events that come into your mind—no matter how silly you think they are. Don't stop until you identify Person B.

4. Now, do anger work at Person B. It is much harder to be angry at this person because it is usually a powerful person from your past. Keep going until you can feel the anger again and let it out. Direct all the "you statements" that you said to Person A to Person B.

5. When you are "clear"—meaning that the anger at Person A is reasonable or proportionate to the event—make clear "I feel" and "I need" statements to Person A.

Example of Anger Work

A woman reported that her husband had been very controlling about whether she should take a cross country trip with another woman without him. She was very angry at him. She was unable to hear any of his concerns. This is an example of the anger work she did.

1. She was clearly feeling "too much" anger at her husband.

2. Starting with the anger she felt at her husband, she said "I am so angry at you. You are so selfish. All you care about is yourself. You don't want me to have a good time. You are mean. You don't trust me. You think I'm too stupid to be able to take care of myself. I hate you."

3. When she asked herself to whom she might say these words, other than her husband, she answered immediately, "My dad."

4. When she tried to do anger work at her father, she found that she could not get angry. She said, "He's old now. He didn't mean the things he said and did." She was willing to continue though because she knew that the anger was "too much" to just be about her husband. Restating the "you statements" she had mentioned earlier, but attributing them to her father, got her in touch with her anger again; and she was

able to do the anger work—at Dad—where it belonged.

She was able to hit the pillows and yell at Dad. She told her father, "You are so mean to me. You don't trust me, and I've never ever done anything to cause you to mistrust me. You are always trying to control me and my friends." She had been triggered by her husband's reluctance and projected her dad onto her husband.

5. When she could clearly see her husband because she had done the anger work, she could also hear his concerns about the age of their car and some of the problems they had with the car. He was able to reassure her that his concerns were because he loved her, not because he didn't trust her. She was able to reassure him that she believed she and her friend could handle anything that might come up with the car. He agreed to spend the money to put new tires on the car sooner than he had planned, so that he would not be worried the whole time about them getting a flat tire.

As you can see, when people get clear about with whom they are dealing, anything is possible. We back ourselves into corners when we react from our feelings before we have processed the root of the feelings.

Does My Butt Look Big?

A Novel Approach to Weight Loss

Read on for an excerpt from the next

Novel/Self-help book

By Jacqueline M. Dierks, Ph.D.

chapter 1

"Does my butt look big in these pants, Sarah?" I asked the question tentatively, because I already knew the answer. Sarah was my best friend in all the world. We'd been friends since high school, and I trusted her implicitly. We had been shopping for hours, and nothing fit in my size. I sure as hell wasn't going to go to the next size up.

"Sammy, what is going on with you? Since I moved out, you have gained a bunch of weight. I've never seen you this heavy—not that you look bad, mind you. I'm not saying that. How much *have* you gained anyway?"

I'm a girl, well actually a woman, but everyone calls me Sam or Sammy. My dad wanted a boy when I was born and though my real name is Samantha no one uses it unless they are mad at me. I've been trying to change that but for the people who have known me forever, I'll probably always be Sammy. "Well," I said sheepishly. "I don't really know. I haven't got a scale—you took it, remember. When you moved out, the scale went with you. It seems like my self-discipline moved out with you, too."

Sarah and I had lived together since we graduated from high school. First we shared a dorm room all the way through college. Then when we graduated, we got an apartment and sort of continued our college lives until *she* met a guy—wouldn't you know it—and ruined everything. She moved in with Tim. I took over our apartment and our dog, Shiloh. It just seems like with Sarah gone, I've turned to food as my new roommate. The size of my butt proves that it actually could act as a roommate—it's big enough now.

"Instead of looking for jeans right now, how about we go shopping for a scale?" Sarah looked at me with her hands on her hips. "Come on, let's go. There's got to be a department store in this mall that sells bathroom scales." Sarah was determined and on a mission.

"I don't want to know." I said weakly. "I know it's bad. I've been shopping for pants like every two months since you left, and I seem to go up a size every time I go shopping. I'm just feeling really frustrated right now, because I absolutely refuse to go up one more size. I'm a pig. I'm a fat pig. I hate my body. I hate myself." I was falling apart on the spot. I started to cry. "I just don't know what to do about it."

Sarah put her arms around me. "You are not a fat pig. Good God, Samantha you are a beautiful woman. You look beautiful right now—just the way you are. There is nothing wrong with your weight, except that *you* aren't happy with it. There is nothing wrong with buying pants a little bigger. You are being really critical of yourself right now. It doesn't help to call yourself names. I do think it would be good to find a scale. It would help you if you knew exactly what you've gained. Maybe then you can make a decision about whether you want to lose anything at all or if you are okay with yourself as you are. Come on, let get out of here."

I was actually really happy to get out of the dressing room. I was sure that the other women had heard my outburst. I bet they were all looking at my butt as I walked out of the dressing room and down the hall. "Let's go get some pretzels." I just love the pretzels at the mall.

Sarah looked at me like I was nuts. "Sammy! For the love of Pete, you were just crying about your weight. Let's just go find a scale and see what's what. Maybe then we can decide what we want to eat."

"Oh crap, you are never any fun. You have always been skinny and always will be. Plus, you got the scale—this is all your fault." I was joking, but only half way. Sarah was perfect. It's hard to be friends with someone who has no problems with anything. She never even had pimples in high school. I knew I was just feeling sorry for myself. Sarah had some terrible problems in her past. Not the least of which was that she lost both her parents in a car accident and had to live with her grandmother from the time she was a freshman in high school. She had moved from the east, and that is when I met her. No, I wasn't being fair. She'd had her issues. She just didn't *look* like she had issues. *Drat!*

"Let's try in here." Sarah said. "They have to have bathroom scales." She was nearly dragging me down the aisles. "There they are." She pointed and we both walked in the direction of the scales. She dragged one down off the shelf and put it on the floor.

"I am *not* stepping on that thing in front of you! I'm not even sure I want to know." I was hissing the words. I knew that I was starting to flip out, and I could see the sales personnel looking our direction.

"Come on, Sam. It's not as bad as you think. Hey, here's one that measures body fat as well as pounds. Do you want that one instead?" She was all sweetness and light.

We had always talked about our weight easily and openly. I knew Sarah wasn't trying to be mean, I just wasn't in the mood for sweet. "Okay, I'm going to kill you right here if you don't quit trying to help so much. Give me the damn scale that measures body fat as well. I might as well know just how big a pig I am." I started to step on the scale when a clerk approached. I literally jumped away from it. If Sarah couldn't know how much I weighed, this little peanut heading for me certainly wasn't going to know.

"Can I be of any help?" She asked politely. "I did notice you were looking at the model that measures body fat. It actually doesn't do that until it's calibrated. You also need to weigh yourself with no clothes on or you won't get an accurate reading."

"Thank God!" I said to myself more than to either one of them. I was off the hook for now.

"I think we'll take this one. We can calibrate it at home. Thanks for your help." Again, Sarah was being Ms. Helpful.

"Yeah! Well, since I'm not going to strip right here, I guess I better take it. Where do I ring it up?" We all walked to the checkout counter. Everyone seemed hunky-dory except for me. *Fat pig*! I thought to myself. *You deserve this humiliation!*

"Sammy, do you want me to come home with you? I'd love to see Shiloh. I miss our baby. I understand if you don't want me to come though. Are you sure you are going to be all right? I feel bad. I feel like I started this whole thing. You aren't mad at me are you?" She was being so nice, almost pleading for forgiveness—for having done nothing wrong, of course.

"No, I don't need you to come home with me. I'm fine, really. You didn't do anything, Sarah. It's just me. I've known for several months that my weight was escalating; I just thought I could get control. One of the women at work asked me to do a weight management program with her. I tried it. It just doesn't work for me. I knew when she asked that I must look like the fat pig I feel like. I know I have to do something. I just don't know what to do. I'll be fine, Sarah, honestly."

"What about going back to Dr. DeWitt? She really helped you with your family. She might be a good person to talk to about this."

"Are you kidding? Nobody goes to a shrink to talk about weight loss. I need a personal trainer or a good diet program. Why would I talk to Maggie—she had asked me to call her that—about gaining weight?"

Sarah looked at me for a minute before continuing. "Sam, you've only started to gain weight since I left. I was just thinking that maybe this is a bigger issue than just not being able to watch what you eat. I'm not saying it is, but if it is, then all the diets in the world aren't going to work. I'm not saying I'm right. I'm just asking you to think about it. I love you. You are my best friend. I don't want to hurt your feelings, but I also want you to be healthy. Please, just think about it."

"Oh, my God!" We both jumped like we'd been shot. "Tim is expecting me home, like now! The time just got away from me. I'm sorry Sammy, but I just have to get home. We made dinner plans with friends and I've got to get ready. We can talk about this more later. Okay? I have *got* to run! Call me! I love it when we get together like this." We exchanged a quick hug and she was gone.

Why is it that when a woman gets involved with a man, their women friends just get shoved to the back? Wait a minute, that's not fair. Sarah makes a lot of time for me given that she is in a relationship. I guess I'm still pissed about the scale. Damn scale! I threw the bag in the back seat with a thud. "Well, this should just be a dandy evening." I said out loud to no one in particular, although the guy getting into the car next to mine did give me the once over. He did not, however, give me a second look—bummer.

I headed home alternately berating myself and feeling sorry for me. Sarah was right. I had never really had a weight problem my whole life. When I lived with her, she did most of the cooking so we ate pretty healthy. It isn't that I don't know *what* to cook. It's more that I don't *want* to cook at all. I eat an awful lot of fast food. Maybe if I just started cooking at home again. *I hate cooking alone. I wish they made a pill I could take and then I wouldn't have to worry about it anymore.*

It is kind of interesting that I've just sort of 'ballooned up.' So what is up with all the weight gain now? Well, I have turned 30. They say that once you turn 30, it is harder to lose weight. I looked at my puffy face in the rearview mirror. "But you aren't even trying to lose weight! You look like a barn." In my own defense I retorted. "Well, aren't you just Little Miss Nasty! Who do you remind me of—could it be Mom?" *Whatever! Now I'm talking like Mom, again.*

As I thought the words, my cell phone rang. It was my mom. *Did I just make this happen by thinking about her? There has to be something to that 'energy' thing some people talk about—if you think about something you make it happen.* I wanted to slap myself—*Quit thinking about your mother. She always shows up when you do. Yikes!*

"Hi, Mom! What's up?" I actually answered the phone as if I weren't half hysterical.

"Samantha, it's Sunday. Are you coming over? I know you never want to come to go to church with us, but are you coming over for dinner? I made chocolate cake. I know it's your favorite. Of course, you probably won't want to eat any because of all the weight you've gained. Anyway, I just wondered if I should set a place for you."

"Sure, Mom, I'll be right over. I'm actually in the car now. I was shopping with Sarah. I'll be there in about 15 minutes. See you soon."

If I ever wondered where the negative messages in my head came from, that call was enough to give me all the insight I needed. My mother has never said a nice thing to me that I can remember. It doesn't matter what I do—it's never good enough. Ever since I was a kid, she would find the negative. If I got a couple of B's in school, I should be getting all A's. If I got all A's, then the courses were too easy and *anybody* could have gotten A's.

I have an older sister and a younger brother. They are the perfect children in my family. My sister Kay did all the right things—went to school, got married, and had kids. She did what my mom expected her to do. I, on the other hand, went to school but haven't found anyone yet and, therefore, have not given her any grandchildren. I really don't think it would matter. My kids would never be as great as Kay's kids.

Brian is my younger brother. He lived with Mom and Dad until recently. He moved in with his girlfriend, Amanda, when they found out she was pregnant. The roof almost came off the house over that one, but Mom has learned to handle it although it's driving her nuts that they won't get married. I hear about it way too much. I can't wait until the baby's born to see if they baptize it. Oh my God! My mother will have a cow if they don't, because she's a traditional Catholic and will be positive the baby is headed for 'limbo' if they don't baptize it. I think the Catholic Church did away with the notion of 'limbo,' but not my mom. It gives her something to be in crisis over, as far as this new baby is concerned—our family sort of lives from one crisis to another.

My dad is another story—sort of a long story at that. He is an alcoholic. He was actively drinking until a few months ago. He's been sober for a while. What's nice is that he actually talks to me about his AA meetings and we are beginning to be friends. He wasn't really very present when I was growing up so this is a nice turn of events. It's our secret that he's in AA. He hasn't told my mom. He will, when he's ready. I'm staying out of the middle of that one.

I pulled up in front of the house. Memories came flooding back. My folks have lived in this house my whole life. It's impossible to come back here without thinking of a million things that happened in this house.

"Samantha, get in here. What took you so long? I thought you said you were only a few minutes away." My mom was yelling out the front door. I'm sure the whole neighborhood could hear. Oh well, they had heard it all before. My mother has no compunction about sharing our family problems with the whole neighborhood. In fact, tomorrow she'll probably go over my visit sentence-by-sentence with Mrs. Flynn who lives next door. They complain about their "problem children" to each other. In my mother's case, I think that she just complains about me. Her other two children are perfect.

"Geez, Mom! I got here as fast as I could. You didn't want me to run stop signs, did you?" *Here I am, feeling defensive before I've even made it to the front door. Some things never change.*

"You look awful! You are as big as a house. No cake for you, young lady!"

"Who is it?" Grandma said, trying to see around my mom.

My grandma lives with my mom and dad. My grandpa died some years ago. Nobody could tolerate my grandpa when he was alive, but now that he's dead—he's a saint. Knowing grandma a little better, now that she's moved in with mom and dad, I think I get why grandpa was such a jerk. Grandma could be mean, and she was especially mean to my mom. Those two had never hit it off, but now under the same roof it was sort of like the 4th of July on a daily basis—fireworks—just sit back and watch them. Fortunately, I could do no wrong when it came to grandma. She loved me just because it made my mom angry.

"Hi, Grandma! How are you?" She was a foot shorter than I was and it seemed like she was getting smaller by the day.

"I'm fine, honey! Same complaints, everything hurts—my knees, my thumbs. I can't knit like I used to, which makes me really mad."

"Yeah, I bet that's hard. And now you have a new great-grandbaby coming. I bet you are really upset about not being able to knit something for Brian's baby."

My mom interrupted. "Oh shush, Sam. Why do you have to create a problem the minute you walk in the door? Let's not talk about that. Come on. Dinner is ready." Kay and Mike were already seated at the table; the kids were nowhere to be seen. *Don't those kids ever eat?* I thought to myself.

My sister practically yelped when I walked in the room. "Wow! Mom said you had gained weight, but I don't think I'd have known you. What's up with that, Sam?"

I detected a gleeful note in my sister's voice. It probably made her heart sing to dig me about my weight. *Bitch!* Her weight probably never fluctuates. She would never allow it. She has to be in total control at all times. "Look, could we get off the subject of my weight, please! I know I've gained a few pounds. I'm taking care of it!" *I am? Wow! That's nice to know. Just how am I doing that? Well, maybe I will call Maggie DeWitt like Sarah suggested.*

"Quit bickering! Come on everyone. Let's eat!" Mom said.

I looked down at the table of food mom had prepared. There was a huge pork roast, mashed potatoes with gravy, dressing, green bean casserole, fruit salad made with real whipped cream, yams with marshmallows on top and, to really top it off, chocolate cake with homemade, butter cream frosting. There is a mini-version of Thanksgiving at my house every Sunday. *Okay, this could be part of my problem. I may as well dig in. Starting tomorrow I'm going on a diet.* "So start passing stuff, you guys. Let's not just sit here looking at it. It's getting cold."

The next morning before heading for work I scrounged around the apartment until I found Maggie DeWitt's card. It had been some time since I had seen her. I felt a little excited about seeing her, but I also felt some trepidation. What would she think of me? I'd gained all this weight since I'd seen her and looked and felt like a cow. To start with, she'd probably think I was crazy calling her about gaining weight. Maybe she would suggest a personal trainer or tell me to try a different weight management program. Even if she did, it would just be good to see her again.

As I drove to work, I was trying to visualize Maggie in my head. I don't think I ever saw a judgmental expression on her face. I was feeling confident that whatever Maggie said or did, it would be supportive and helpful. Once I got to my desk, I picked up the phone and dialed it.

"Dr. DeWitt's office, can I help you?" It was the same pleasant-sounding woman who had been the office manager when I saw Maggie in the past.

"Hi! This is Samantha Daley. I was Dr. DeWitt's client some months back. I was wondering if I could make an appointment with her? I don't know if you remember, but I usually did lunch-hour appointments." I felt relief. I was doing something for myself.

"Of course I remember you, Samantha. She has an opening this Friday at 11:30. Will that work for you?"

"That will work great for me. I'll see you then."

"Don't forget to bring your insurance card. It will be good to see you, again." She said as she hung up.

Whew! I feel a sense of relief, just knowing that I had called and that I would be seeing Maggie this week. I also took a moment to congratulate myself. I had done it! I had learned so much the last time that I worked with Maggie. I was actually excited about beginning again with a new "project"—my weight.

Author Biography

JACQUELINE M. DIERKS, Ph.D., LCSW, earned her doctorate in Clinical Social Work at Arizona State University. Her thesis "The Effects of a Personal Empowerment Program Upon the Perceived Self-Efficacy of Women in Social Situations," developed a treatment program for women confronting the limitations placed on them by society. A former instructor at ASU, she is a published author and frequent trainer at workshops for therapists. Dr. Dierks has been a member of the mental health field since 1984 and is in private practice, where her focus is primarily on women's issues.

Pg 44

CPSIA information can be obtained
at www.ICGtesting.com
Printed in the USA
FSOW02n1152080118
43175FS